TRUE
Mystery
STORIES

TRUE
Mystery
STORIES

FINN BEVAN

Robinson Children's Books

Robinson Publishing Ltd
7 Kensington Church Court
London W8 4SP

First published in the UK by Robinson Children's
Books, an imprint of Robinson Publishing Ltd 1997

A copy of the British Library Cataloguing in
Publications data is available from the British Library.

ISBN 1 85487 456 X

Printed and bound in the UK

1 3 5 7 9 10 8 6 4 2

Contents

Chapter 5

RIDDLES OF THE PAST

Chapter 6

UNIDENTIFIED FLYING OBJECTS

Chapter 7

GHOSTS AND HAUNTINGS

Chapter 8

MYSTERY NEWS

CHAPTER 1

MYSTERY PEOPLE

DID THE ROMANOVS REALLY DIE?

On the night of 16 July 1918, the last Tsar of Russia, Nicholas II, his wife, the Tsarina Alexandra, their son Alexei and their four beautiful daughters – Olga, Tatiana, Maria and Anastasia – were ordered by their guards into the cellar of the house they occupied in the small mining town of Ekaterinburg. Early in the previous year, Russia had been torn apart by violent revolution and Nicholas had been forced to abdicate while a new government, made up mainly of left-wing revolutionaries, took over the running of the country. The Tsar and his family had been held prisoner, for their own safety, first in their own palace in St Petersburg, and more recently in the commandeered home of a Professor Nikolai Ipatiev in Ekaterinburg. Here they were kept behind specially built fences, under the watchful eyes of fifty armed guards. Now, after months of hiding and uncertainty, they dared to hope for the first time that their ordeal was nearing its end. They had been told that they were no longer safe in Ekaterinburg and were about to be evacuated to Czechoslovakia. There was an air of excitement and expectation which they had not felt for a very long time. In his arms, the Tsar gently carried the 13-year old Alexei, his only son and heir. For Alexei suffered from the hereditary disease of haemophilia which prevented his blood from clotting; a single scratch or bump could prove fatal to the young prince. The Tsar was given a chair to sit on. And then, as quickly as it had appeared, all hope was extinguished. Their gaoler, a Siberian Jew, called Yurovsky, spoke to the Tsar:

"Nicholas Alexandrovich, your followers have tried to save your life. But they have failed and have sealed your fate. You and your family will be shot."

"What did you say?" the Tsar stuttered, disbelieving. "What did you say?"

"Words cannot save you now," Yurovsky replied and shot the Tsar in the chest with a revolver. As he slumped from the chair, dead, his wife and family fell to their knees in front of Yurovsky.

"Have mercy on my children," the Tsarina begged her husband's murderer. "Do what you will with my life, but spare my children, I beseech you. They have done nothing wrong."

Her words fell on deaf ears. The Tsarina, her children, their doctor, cook and two servants, were shot where they knelt. Outside a lorry revved up its engine to hide the noise of the gunshots.

Just a few days later, the town was taken by the White Russian army, whose soldiers remained faithful the Tsar and bitterly opposed to the Bolshevik revolutionaries who had brought him down, and an investigation was ordered into the terrible events of that July night. The account above is based on the findings of that investigation.

But just how far was the investigation to be believed? What had actually happened on that fateful night? The investigation was dismissed by some people as propaganda put about by the White Russians to gain maximum support for the Tsar. To back up their claim, the White Russians produced photographs which claimed to show the cellar complete with bullet holes in the walls and floors hastily scrubbed clean of bloodstains. Another official statement, issued a few days after the murder by the other side, however, claimed that while the Tsar had indeed been killed, his wife and son had been spared and sent away to a safe place. The official bulletin read:

"The family of Romanov has been taken to another and safer place."

Yet another report repeated the claim that

the Tsar was dead but this time added that the rest of the royal family, his daughters included, had been sent away to safety. What was the truth of the matter? Did the Romanov royal family really die in the Ekaterinburg cellar, or did some of them survive? It was the beginning of one of the most intriguing mysteries of the twentieth century. The main problem facing investigators of the case was lack of evidence. No bodies were ever found to back up what they believed to have happened. Until 1995, when DNA tests on bones found in a grave in woods outside Moscow proved to be the remains of those of the Romanov family. However, it was not clear whether *all* the bones belonged to the Tsar's family, so exactly what happened to all the children is still something of a mystery.

And the question remained – if any of the children had survived the massacre, where did they go to afterwards? The day after the murders, a train was seen leaving Ekaterinburg station with its blinds firmly pulled down, bound for an unknown destination. But the identity of its passengers remained a closely-guarded secret . . .

And now comes perhaps the strangest part of this mysterious tale. The Tsar's youngest daughter, Anastasia, was 17 years old in July 1918. Two years later, in February 1920, an unknown young woman tried to commit suicide by jumping into a canal in Berlin, Germany. The police issued the following bulletin to the press:

"Yesterday evening at 9 p.m. a girl of about twenty jumped off the Bendler Bridge into the Landwehr Canal with the intention of taking her own life. She was saved by a police sergeant and admitted to the Elisabeth Hospital in Lutzow-strasse. No papers or valuables of any kind were found in her possession, and she refused to make any statement about herself or her

motives for attempting suicide."

Unable to find out who the girl was or the reasons why she wanted to end her life, the authorities sent her to a local mental home where she remained for two years, refusing to answer questions about herself or to take part in anything that was going on around her. And here the mystery deepened further. A fellow patient, who had lived in Moscow before the revolution, claimed to recognize the girl as the Grand Duchess Tatiana, the Tsar's second eldest daughter. Some months later, a retired police official, Baron Arthur von Kleist, befriended "Tatiana" and took her to live in his own home. As the girl learned to trust her benefactor, she opened up to him and began to tell him about her past life. During one of their many conversations, she told Baron von Kleist that she was indeed a Romanov, as the woman had guessed, but that she was not Tatiana. She was in fact the Grand Duchess Anastasia, the Tsar's youngest daughter. She said that she had been present at the massacre of her family in Ekaterinburg but that she had been rescued by one of the soldiers present that night and had travelled with him and his family to Romania. When he died, she drifted to Berlin and there, friendless and without any family, she decided to end her miserable life.

Though the girl and her sensational story attracted a huge amount of attention all over Europe, not everyone was taken in by her claim. The Tsarina's sister, Anastasia's aunt, came to see her but did not believe her to be her niece. She was an imposter, the aunt announced, though not a malicious one. On the other hand, her uncle, the Grand Duke Andrei, who had known Anastasia better than her aunt, was convinced that the mystery girl was telling the truth. And various other acquaintances, including the daughter of the royal doctor, were said to be sure of her identity — Anastasia told the doctor's daughter that she clearly remembered being treated by the doctor for measles, recalling details which no one other than herself and her sisters could possibly have known.

In 1938, "Anastasia" was finally persuaded by a German lawyer, to try officially to prove her true identity once and for all and to establish her right to her share of her father's surviving fortune. The attempt lasted for more than twenty years, becoming one of the longest legal cases in history, but eventually ended in failure, partly on account of the evidence given by an Austrian man who claimed to have been an eyewitness to the massacre. As the years passed, it became increasingly impossible to unravel the truth of the matter or to verify Anastasia's true identity. Then, in 1967, the woman who claimed to be Anastasia married Dr John Manahan, a former professor of history, and settled in Charlottesville, USA, under the assumed name, Anna Anderson. Her husband shielded her from much unwelcome publicitiy, although visitors continued to call on her, in an effort to solve once and for all the mystery of the Ekaterinburg cellar. Anna Anderson would never say for certain what happened that night. Surely if she had been there she could have put an end to the mystery of what happened to the Romanovs, once and for all? Anna Anderson died in early 1984, well into her eighties, the subject of two feature films, many books and numerous newspaper and magazine articles, her true identity still unknown and the fate of the Romanovs still a matter of speculation. Was she in fact the Grand Duchess Anastasia, as she claimed to be? Or had that young girl died many years before, in a hail of revolutionaries' bullets?

Postscript: Recent DNA tests seem to prove that Anna Anderson was *not* a Romanov, but the results are by no means universally accepted and the mystery lives on ...

WHO WAS ROBIN HOOD?

Robin Hood, champion of the poor and notorious outlaw, is one of the most famous and best-loved heroes of British legend. But did such a man actually exist? Was he a real person who lived in Sherwood Forest with his loyal band of followers, robbing from the rich to give to the poor and engaged in a long and bitter feud with the Sheriff of Nottingham? Or was he a figure of myth and legend, and nothing more? What do you think? Here are some facts and theories to help you make up your mind.

The Case for Robin Hood –
fact or fiction?

· The earliest ballads telling of Robin Hood's adventures were being sung as early as the 14th century. His fame spread further with the publication of a pamphlet called "A Lytell Geste of Robyn Hood", printed in 1510.

· In Sir Walter Scott's famous work "Ivanhoe" (1847), Robin Hood is a great friend and ally of Richard the Lionheart.

· Some scholars think that Robin Hood was really Robin Wood, a name linked with the great Norse god, Wodin.

· Others think that he was a real outlaw who lived in Sherwood Forest in the thirteenth century.

· He may have been a nobleman who turned to crime because he was unhappy at the way in which the poor and needy were treated. Two possible contenders for his true identity are Sir Robin of Locksley (in Yorkshire) and the Earl of Huntingdon.

· In the Middle Ages, Sherwood Forest stretched from Nottinghamshire north into Yorkshire, backing up the claim that Robin Hood and Robin of Locksley were one and the same person.

- In the 1850s, another important clue came to light. An ancient, historic document was found giving details of a forester, Robert Hood, the son of Adam Hood. He was born in 1280 and lived with his wife, Matilda, in Wakefield, Yorkshire. For Robert and Matilda, read Robin and Maid Marian?

- The record goes on to say that Robert Hood was fined for not joining the king's army to fight against the Scots. Some years later, however, he seems to have fought with the Earl of Lancaster, this time against the king himself (Edward II). The rebels were defeated, the Earl beheaded, and his followers declared to be outlaws. Did Robert Hood then flee to the forest, to avoid being caught?

- According to one story, the king became such a staunch admirer of Robin Hood that he not only forgave him for poaching deer from the royal forest but invited him to join the royal household. Robin stayed in his service for about a year, working as a gentleman of the royal bedchamber. He was then granted permission to return home for a few days but he never came back to court when his leave was up. Instead, he lived out the rest of his days in the forest with his band of merry men.

· Robin Hood had many followers among the poor. England's forests were once common land where anyone could hunt for rabbit and deer to eat. In the Middle Ages, the forests were declared to be the king's own private property and there were strict penalties for anyone caught trespassing or poaching. Robin regularly broke these, in his eyes unjust, laws, killing deer to feed himself and to give to the poor peasants who lived nearby.

· Many more legends surround Robin Hood's death. According to one story, he fell ill and went to the Abbey of Kirklees to be bled. In those days, this was a common, cure-all treatment for many types of illnesses. The Prioress decided to take her revenge for the many wealthy churchmen Robin had robbed, and let him bleed to death.

· Robin is said to have buried in the Abbey grounds, within a bowshot of the walls.

· In the nineteenth century, the tombstone which was supposed to mark his grave was broken up by workmen building a nearby railway. There were rumours that it had magical powers.

WHAT KILLED NAPOLEON?

By the time Napoleon died in exile on the island of St Helena on 5 May 1821, at the age of 52, he was a very sick man indeed. He had grown fat and flabby, suffered from frequent bouts of depression, was constantly cold but suffered from headaches if he stayed out in bright sunlight for too long. He also suffered painfully from gout. But the nature of the illness that finally killed him has never been established for certain. On the day after his death, a team of seven doctors gathered to watch Napoleon's personal physician, Dr Francesco Antommarchi, perform an autopsy on his body. The doctors were unable to agree among themselves about the results of the autopsy and submitted four different reports about the cause of Napoleon's death. Dr Antommarchi himself concluded that Napoleon had died from stomach cancer, and this is the opinion which was generally accepted for many years afterwards.

Napoleon himself had been in no doubt about what, or who, was making him ill. A few weeks before he died, he added the following

words to his last will and testament:

"I die prematurely, murdered by the English oligarchy and its hired assassin."

The former emperor, in his heyday, the most powerful man in Europe, was convinced that his old enemy, the English, and more particularly, the British governor of St Helena, Hudson Lowe – the "hired assassin" of his will – were trying to kill him. For it was the British who had sentenced him to exile on St Helena, following their crushing victory over him at the Battle of Waterloo. A small, bleak, extinct volcano, the island of St Helena lies in the South Atlantic Ocean about 15 degrees south of the Equator. Its main use was as a stopping place for trading ships travelling between India and England on behalf of the British East India Company. It was here that they took on supplies of fresh water for the long voyage ahead. And it was here that Napoleon arrived in 1815, to end his days. He was accompanied by a force of two thousand British troops who had been sent to guard him and a small group of close friends and personal servants to keep him company. Among his companions was his lifelong friend, Henri-Gratien Bertrand, and a more recent aquaintance, Count Charles-Tristan de Montholon. The former emperor and his entourage were lodged in Longwood House, a large villa situated in the hills some way from the port. It was a dreary, uncomfortable place, infested with rats and riddled with damp. Napoleon's existence was equally dreary, a far cry from the life of glamour and luxury that he had enjoyed in Paris. He spent most of his time dictating his memoirs to his secretary or reliving great military glories of days gone by. The evenings were spent playing chess or cards, or reading – every day the same as the day before.

On 14 April 1816, a new governor arrived at St Helena. His name was Major General Sir

Hudson Lowe. He and Napoleon disliked and distrusted each other intensely from the moment Lowe was introduced to his famous prisoner. Lowe was terrifed that Napoleon might try, or be helped, to escape from St Helena and he went to great lengths to ensure that this did not happen. The guard on Napoleon was redoubled, his letters were censored and visitors to Longwood House kept to a minimum.

"Why don't you just go ahead and assassinate me, since that is obviously your intention!" Napoleon stormed at his final meeting with Lowe.

"The English are not assassins," Lowe replied coolly. But Napoleon remained unconvinced. His friend, Bertrand, took up his cause. He wrote to Lowe, requesting him to allow the former emperor greater freedom of movement. He would not survive long otherwise, Bertrand concluded. But his request went unanswered and unheeded.

Now Napoleon became convinced that the British, at Lowe's command, were slowly poisoning him. In his diary of 19 July 1820, his physician, Dr Antommarchi, seemed to agree with his famous patient. He noted that Napoleon was suffering from "shivering, fever, pain in the head, nausea, dry and frequent coughing, and vomiting of a bilious quality", all of which symptoms marked the beginning of a slow, debilitating illness which eventually killed Napoleon less than a year later.

But what was it that finally killed Napoleon? Were his suspicions correct? Or were they merely the deluded ramblings of an exhausted and defeated man? In the years following Napoleon's death, his devoted valet, Louis Marchand, wrote his own account of the former emperor's final days in his memoirs. The book was not published until 1955. It soon came to the attention of a Swedish expert on poisons, Sven Forshufvud. Dr Forshufvud read the memoirs with great interest and reached the same conclusion as Napoleon – that the former emperor had been the victim of arsenic poisoning. But, he concluded, the murderer had not been the much-hated Hudson Lowe, but a member of Napoleon's own entourage – the Count de Montholon, acting on behalf of the French monarchy who wished to get rid of Napoleon and re-establish their own rights to the French throne. According to Dr Forshufvud, Montholon, who also acted as Napoleon's wine steward, administered the poison in the emperor's daily ration of wine. Napoleon drank half a bottle of South African wine, of which he had his own private supply, with each meal. At other times, the wine was kept in a locked cupboard, to which only Montholon had the key.

In 1982, an English chemist put forward another, rather more bizarre theory about the cause of Napoleon's death. While agreeing that Napoleon died of arsenic poisoning, he blamed not the contaminated wine but the green dye in the wallpaper which decorated the drawing room of Longwood House. The pigment that gave the green its colour was found to contain arsenic. Rather than being the result of a carefully calculated plot, could Napoleon's death have been brought about accidentally by toxic vapours from the wallpaper? We will never know for sure. Whoever, or whatever, killed Napoleon, the facts of arsenic poisoning seem to be indisputable. Indeed, when Napoleon's body was exhumed (dug up) on St Helena in 1840, to be taken back to France for a belated state burial, a shock awaited those who watched the coffin being opened. Despite the passage of the years, the former emperor's body was in remarkable condition, thanks maybe to the peculiar preservative powers of all the arsenic to which he had been subjected during his exile.

WHO WAS THE MONA LISA?

The face of the Mona Lisa smiles mysteriously down from the wall of the Louvre art gallery in Paris. But who was the model for Leonardo's famous masterpiece? The original sitter for the portrait, which took Leonardo four years to complete, was Mona Lisa del Giocondo, the wife of a Florentine nobleman. Her sad smile masked a personal tragedy, for, at the time of the sitting, she was still in mourning for the death of her baby daughter. Leonardo left the portrait in the hands of the Giocondo family when he had finished it.

Shortly afterwards, however, Leonardo was asked by Guiliano de Medici to paint a portrait of his mistress, Constanza d'Avalos. She not only looked like the original Mona Lisa but, by a strange coincidence, she had been given the nickname, "La Gioconda", which means "Smiler". Leonardo was known to do two or more versions of each portrait he painted, and he may well have adapted one of the original versions of the Mona Lisa, replacing the face with that of Constanza d'Avalos. By the time it was finished, however, Guiliano de Medici had grown tired of Constanza and did not buy the portrait from Leonardo.

So whose face is it that smiles down from the Louvre wall – the original Mona Lisa or La Gioconda? Opinions are divided. But some experts think that, when Leonardo left Italy for France some time later, he took the unwanted portrait of Constanza with him and

that it is La Gioconda whose face adorns the walls of the Louvre, while the real Mona Lisa later found its way from Florence to England and now belongs to a private collector in London.

Did you know? There are more than sixty alleged versions of the Mona Lisa in existence around the world.

WHO WAS THE MAN IN THE IRON MASK?

The Daily Mystery

20 November 1703

Speculation mounted today about the identity of the mysterious, masked prisoner who died last night in the Bastille prison, Paris, after a short illness. He had been in prison for thirty four years. The dead man will be buried later today, as Monsieur Marchioly, a false name since his real name remains unknown.

According to his guards, the prisoner was a man of high rank (even the prisoner governor stood in his presence), tall and well built, with a taste for fine linen and good books. No one, not even his gaolers, ever glimpsed his face, however, nor discovered his true identity. For he always wore a mask, some say of iron, some say of black velvet, which he never removed, even to eat. Two musketeers remained constantly by his side, with orders to kill him if he ever took this extraordinary contraption off. Otherwise, the prisoner seems to have been well treated and to have been given everything he asked for.

But who was this mystery man? Rumours that he was King Louis XIV himself have been strenuously denied by the king's private office. He arrived at the Bastille in 1698, when Monsieur St Mars, took over as prison governor. Since then, every precaution possible has been taken to prevent him being recognized. Monsieur St Mars was unavailable for comment today but a former employee at the Bastille, who wishes to remain nameless, has been helping the paper with our enquiries. According to this source, the mask was more of a precaution than a punishment. Why this should be so, we do not know. Could it be that the stranger bore a marked resemblance to a famous figure – a resemblance which could have proved an embarassment if it ever came to light?

One theory is that the prisoner was none other than the real father of our present king. As readers of this paper will know, there was much surprise in 1638 when Queen Anne of Austria (wife of Louis XIII, our present king's official father) gave birth to a son, long after the royal couple had abandoned hope of producing an heir. It was also no secret that the royal couple loathed the sight of each other and had lived apart for many years. Then, as now, rumours abounded about the identity of the baby's real father, perhaps a handsome young nobleman of royal descent, only too willing to help the king and queen out of their dilemma? If this suggestion is true, did our present king's real father return from exile abroad, only to find himself a source of royal embarassment? Since killing his own father was clearly out of the question, the king would have had no option but to keep him hidden away, in comfort but cut off from human con-

tact. Another related theory is that the stranger was the king's illegitimate brother, locked away once again to conceal his physical resemblance to King Louis XIV.

Yet another theory about the stranger's identity is that he was a man called Eustache Dauger. An importance piece of evidence which seems to back this up is a letter written on behalf of the

King to Monsieur St Mars, some time before the masked man arrived at the Bastille.

The letter read:

"The King has commanded that I am to have this man named Eustache Dauger sent to you. It is of the utmost importance. . .that he should be securely guarded and that he should in no way give information about himself or send any letters. . .You must on no account listen to what he may want to say to you, but threaten to kill him if he opens his mouth."

Strong words indeed! The letter makes one thing quite clear – this Eustache Dauger knew some secret so astonishing that the king himself wished it concealed. But why did the king not kill Dauger, and his secret with him? Who was Eustache Dauger and what had he done? After extensive research, our reporter can now exclusively reveal that he was none other than Eustache Dauger de Cavoye, the son of a captain in the royal guard and brother of one of the king's most trusted officials. Eustache and his brothers were brought up at court and were childhood playmates of the king (a fact which may later have saved Eustache's life). In 1659, while still only in his twenties,

Eustache was apparently involved in a series of bizarre incidents. He took part in a black mass, causing a tremendous scandal among polite society, and he later killed a page-boy in a drunken brawl. For this, he was stripped of his military rank. Details for the next few years are sketchy but, by 1672, it seems, Eustache had already spent some time in prison. Rumour has it that the final straw in his chequered career was his involvement in the notorious "affair of poisons" in which a group of wealthy ladies poisoned, or attempted to poison, their husbands after taking part in black masses. More scandalous still was the involvement of the king's mistress in scenes of sorcery and witchcraft so sinister that they could only be investigated in the utmost secrecy. It seems likely that Eustache Dauger was in some way implicated in these shocking events and was arrested by special order of the king as he attempted to flee to England.

Whoever the stranger was, and we shall probably never know for sure, he was no common prisoner. Dangerous enough to be locked away for over thirty years, the threat he posed to the king must have been a very real one indeed. But there are no records of any person of rank or military importance going missing during this time. One thing is for certain – his crime or his potential for crime must have been very great. While in prison on the Ile Sainte Marguerite, before his transfer to the Bastille, so the story goes, the masked man scratched a few words on a plate and threw them out of the window of his prison cell. A local fisherman picked up the plate and took it to the prison governor.

"Have you read what is written here?" the governor asked the fisherman.

" No," the man answered. "I cannot read."

"Then you are lucky. . ." was the governor's sinister reply.

CHAPTER 2

LOST LANDS

DID ATLANTIS SINK INTO THE SEA?

In about 350 BC, the Greek author and philosopher, Plato, wrote of a great island in the Atlantic Ocean which, in the space of a day and a night, had vanished without trace beneath the waves. This was the story of the lost continent of Atlantis which remains as much of a mystery today as it did in Plato's time, more than 2,000 years ago.

Plato's two great works about Atlantis were called *Timaeus* and *Critias*. In his version of events, Plato puts the story into the mouth of the Athenian, Critias, who tells the tale as one which he heard from his grandfather, who in turn heard it from a sixth-century wise man, called Solon. In his turn, Solon was thought to have heard the story from an Egyptian priest who said that it all happened a very long time ago, even by Ancient Egyptian standards. This is the account of Atlantis given by the Egyptian priest and reported by Plato in *Timaeus*:

> *"Many great and wonderful deeds are recorded of your state (Athens) in our histories. But one of them exceeds all the rest in great-*

*ness and valour. For these histories tell of a
mighty power which unprovoked made an
expedition against the whole of Europe and
Asia, and to which your city put an end. This
power came forth out of the Atlantic Ocean, for
in those days the Atlantic was navigable; and
there was an island situated in front of the
straits which are by you called the Pillars of
Hercules. The island was larger than Libya
and Asia put together, and was the way to
other islands, and from these you might pass
to the whole of the opposite continent which
surrounded the true ocean; for this sea which
is within the Straits of Hercules (that is, the
Mediterranean) is only a harbour, having a
narrow entrance, but that other is a real sea,
and the land surrounding it on every side may
be most truly called a boundless continent.
Now in this island of Atlantis there was a
great and wonderful empire which had rule
over the whole island and several others, and
over parts of the continent, and furthermore,
the men of Atlantis had subjected the parts of
Libya within the columns of Heracles (the
Straits of Gibraltar) as far as Egypt, and of
Europe as far as Tyrrhenia (northern Italy).
This vast power, gathered into one, endeav-
oured to subdue at a blow our country (Egypt)
and yours (Greece) and the whole of the region*

*within the Straits; and then, Solon, your coun-
try defeated and triumphed over the invaders,
and preserved from slavery those who were not
yet subjugated, and generously liberated all
the rest of us who dwelt within the Pillars. But
afterwards here occurred violent earthquakes
and floods; and in a single day and night of
misfortune all your warlike men in a body
sank into the earth, and the island of Atlantis
in like manner disappeared in the
depths of the sea . . ."*

What was this amazing city like? In his
second work, *Critias*, Plato describes it in
much greater detail. He says that the city was
circular in shape and built around a hill, or
acropolis. A magnificent royal palace stood on
top of the hill. The palace had the rare and
unusual feature of fountains which ran with
hot and cold water. The king who lived in the
palace hunted royal bulls in the temple
precinct. On ceremonial occasions, he dressed
in fabulous azure-blue robes. An exquisite
temple to Poseidon, god of the sea and of
Atlantis, stood in the precinct:

*"All the outside of the temple, with the exception
of the pinnacles, they covered with silver, and the
pinnacles with gold. In the interior of the temple,
the roof was of ivory, adorned everywhere with gold*

*and silver and other precious metals. All the other
parts of the walls and pillars and floor were lined
with precious metals. In the temple they placed
statues of gold; there was the god (Poseidon) himself standing in a chariot – the charioteer of six
winged horses – and of such a size that he touched
the roof of the building with his head . . ."*

The civilization which had built this splendid place was no less extraordinary, according
to Plato. They were a golden people in a golden
place. And then, one day, in the space of twenty
four hours, their golden world came crashing
down around them. They had sinned against
the great god, Zeus, and his revenge was swift.
He destroyed the entire continent, its golden
people and its palaces.

But what really caused Atlantis to sink
beneath the sea in such a dramatic way? Ever
since Plato's time, the fate of Atlantis has
gripped people's imaginations in a way few
places ever have, and a whole host of theories,
sensible and bizarre, have grown up about the
lost city. The modern revival of interest in the
fate of Atlantis came in the nineteenth century, with the publication of an extraordinary
book, *Atlantis, the Antediluvian World*, written by the American writer and politician,
Ignatius Donnelly. It became a best seller and

the cult of Atlantis was born. While many scholars dismissed Atlantis as make-believe, Donnelly argued that there really had been a lost continent in the Atlantic Ocean, to the west of the Straits of Gibraltar and that it had perished in the exact manner described by Plato. He believed not only that Atlantis had existed but that it had been the cradle of all civilisation, where mankind had first come into being. He backed up his theory with numerous zoological and geological theories and statistics. Donnelly concluded that Atlantis may have been destroyed by a real, natural disaster, such as an earthquake or volcanic eruption. Unfortunately, his work was all based on pure speculation. There was not a single shred of hard evidence to back it up. But it was fascinating, there was no doubt about it!

Donnelly's book whetted people's appetites and imaginations. In the following years, hundreds more books were written about Atlantis and hundreds more theories, each one more outrageous than the last, were put forward. Here are just a few of the more bizarre and unusual of the facts and theories:

- The Russian writer, Helena Blavatsky, claimed that the people of Atlantis were the fourth race on Earth, with amazing psychic powers. But they were corrupted by the great dragon King Thevetat and were turned into wicked magicians. They began a war which ended with their complete destruction.
- Madame Blavatsky also suggested that the survivors of the disaster had gone on to become the Ancient Egyptians and had built the pyramids!
- Another so called scholar claimed to have been able to read the ancient psychic records of Atlantis. He deduced that while

some of the Atlantians had certainly moved to Egypt, some other survivors of the disaster travelled to England where they built Stonehenge.

. In the nineteenth century, the British Prime Minister, William Gladstone, was so fascinated by the story of Atlantis that he even asked Parliament for funds so that he could send an expedition to find the lost continent. (Needless to say, his request was turned down!)

. The English explorer, Colonel Percy H. Fawcett was convinced that Brazil was part of ancient Atlantis and, in 1924, he set off to find the ruins of the continent's long-lost cities hidden deep in the Brazilian jungle. He was never seen again.

. In 1940, a psychic, Edgar Cayce, predicted that Atlantis would rise again from the sea in 1968 or 1969 somewhere near the Bahamas. It didn't, and the world is still waiting . . .

. In the 1950s, one of the best selling books about Atlantis was Worlds in Collision by another Russian, Immanuel Velikovsky. The author suggested that Atlantis had been destroyed when a comet collided with it. (He also blamed comets for causing the great flood of the Bible,

among other things. You can read another
version of what caused the Biblical flood
on page 188.)
- Some of the locations suggested for
Atlantis include Sri Lanka, Greenland,
Mexico, the Sahara Desert and South
Africa.
- In 1975, a special conference was held at
the University of Indiana, USA, to debate
the question: Atlantis, fact or fiction? A
team of experts reached the conclusion
that Atlantis was a myth. But even experts
can be wrong!

So, is there any truth at all behind the story of
Atlantis? It seems that there might be. In the
1960s, a Greek archaeologist suggested that a
gigantic volcanic explosion, which had ripped
apart the Greek island of Thera (Santorini) in
1500 BC, had also destroyed Atlantis. The
explosion also destroyed the civilizations of
northern Crete and of the eastern part of the
mainland. Before the explosion, Thera had
been a large, round island, corresponding to
Plato's description of Atlantis. So huge was
the explosion that destroyed it, that even
today, large parts of the remaining island are
covered in thick layers of volanic ash.
Subsequent excavations have revealed the

remains of houses with sophisticated plumbing systems (remember the hot and cold fountains?) and beautifully decorated with frescos, showing among other things, the sport of bull-leaping (remember the King of Atlantis?). It was obvious that the Therans, like the Atlantians, had been part of a very advanced civilisation. Were they one and the same? – we will never know.

The only thing we can say for certain is that we are no nearer to solving the mystery of Atlantis today than Plato was thousands of years ago. Even in Plato's time, the whole, incredible story of Atlantis was based on rumour and hearsay which was already hundreds of years old. And nothing has really changed. But there is still something magical in the thought that, lying somewhere deep beneath the Atlantic waves, are the ruins of one of the greatest and most fabulous cities that ever existed. The fascination of the lost continent of Atlantis shows no signs of fading.

WAS THE LOST GOLD OF EL DORADO EVER FOUND?

In 1532, just thirteen years after Hernando Cortes and his army of Spanish conquistadors had plundered the vast golden treasures of the Aztec emperor, Montezuma, another group of Spaniards arrived in South America. They were led by a soldier called Francisco Pizarro. Like Cortes before him, Pizarro had one thing on his mind – he wanted gold, and he wanted plenty of it. Pizarro's quest led him to Peru where, thanks to their superior weaponry, he and his army entered the great empire of the Incas almost unopposed. He led his men across the narrow coastal plain and up the rough, winding road that snaked high into the Andes Mountains. In the city of Caxamalca, the Spaniards were met by the Inca ruler, Atahuallpa. Atahuallpa greeted them cordially, as Montezuma had before him. But the Spaniards ignored his courtesies, killed his followers without mercy and took the emperor prisoner. They kept him locked inside one of the city's temples while they plundered the royal palace and the city treasury, looting every piece of gold and precious jewellery they could find.

When Atahuallpa heard of the Spaniard's insatiable greed for gold, he decided to try and buy his way out of captivity. He said that if Pizarro set him free, he would fill the room he was kept in with gold as high as Pizarro could reach. Pizarro was hooked. He had seen the golden roofs of the city and walked over floors inlaid with gold. This was an offer beyond his wildest dreams. Quickly, he agreed to the emperor's terms, gave him two months to fulfil his promise, then sat back to watch his dreams come true. At the emperor's command, gold began to pour into the city from all corners of the empire – from temples, palaces and noble houses. The Spaniards watched delightedly as the room was piled high with glittering gold. When it was full, they lost no time in ruthlessly melting the gold down and shipping it back to Spain. Their fortunes were assured. But Pizarro had no intention of keeping his side of the bargain. He forced the emperor to convert to Christianity, then he executed him. The Spanish plunder of the Inca empire had only just begun . . .

Despite the vast quantities of gold they were given or which they plundered and stole, the

Spanish were never satisfied. They wanted more, and more. The lust for gold led them to believe any number of stories about fabulous treasures hidden in the mountains beyond the Inca lands. One of the strangest, and most tantalizing, tales of all was the legend of El Dorado, not the "Golden Land" as many people thought, but the "Golden Man". Rumours of El Dorado reached the ears of one of Pizarro's soldiers, Sebastian Benalcazar, in 1535, on his travels around South America. This is the story he heard:

Far away in the Andes Mountains, in the country we know today as Columbia, there lived a peace-loving people called the Chibcha. Deep within their lands lay a beautiful sacred lake, called Guatavita. According to legend, a golden god lived in the lake, having descended from the sky, which is why the lake was sacred. Each year, an extraordinary ceremony was performed on the lake. The ruler of the Chibcha was rowed into the middle of the lake, on a golden raft laden with gold and emeralds. There he stripped off his robes and smeared his body with a sticky substance, like glue. He was then covered in gold dust, so that his whole body glistened and shone like the sun. This was El Dorado – the Golden Man. Then the ruler threw the gold and precious jewels which filled his raft into the lake, as offerings to the god. Finally, he bathed in the sacred waters, to wash the gold dust away and to gain some of the lake's sacred powers for his people.

The Spanish explorers were fascinated by the story of El Dorado, and longed to find the sacred lake and take its untold riches for themselves. "Who knows?" they reasoned. "If there was a golden lake, why not a whole golden city?" Their greed knew no bounds. Within a matter of a few years, several expeditions had been mounted to find the lake. But the Chibcha people had by now gone from the region, and with them all knowledge of the ritual. Those who were left were brutally tortured and killed as the Spanish tried to force them to give up their secret treasures. The lake itself was even more unyielding. Nestled among the mountains, and shrouded in mist, its air of mystery tantalized and infuriated the Spanish gold-diggers. The only solution, they decided, was to drain the lake and dredge the treasures out of it. In 1544, a soldier, Herman Perez de Qesada, organized the first attempt to drain the lake. He formed the local people into teams to carry out his plan of emptying the lake with buckets but after sev-

eral months of back-breaking work, the water level had only dropped a few feet. De Qesada could see a small collection of golden objects in the shallow water around the lakeside but he could get no further. In 1578, a Spanish merchant, Antonio de Sepulveda, made a more elaborate attempt to solve the mystery. He commanded eight thousand local people to dig a huge channel through the lake's crater-like rim. Millions of gallons of water poured out, enough to uncover many priceless golden offerings and an exquisite emerald the size of an egg. But De Sepulveda's joy was short lived.

The pressure of the water flowing out of the lake caused the sides of the channel to cave in. Hundreds of people were killed and work was abandoned.

Explorers continued to be spell-bound by the mystery of El Dorado but none ever found a way to make the lake spill its secrets. Many came, tried and failed. Many perished in the attempt. The legend lived on. It even came to the attention of the great British explorer, Sir Walter Raleigh who wrote of it in the late sixteenth century and clearly became obsessed by the notion that a golden city lay undiscovered beneath the water. In 1595, he set out to find El Dorado but, like so many before him, he came back empty-handed. Many years later, in the early 1900s, another attempt was made to drain the lake, by a British company of contractors. They drained the lake from underneath, by boring upwards into its crater. But the mud which covered the exposed lake bed was so soft that no one could walk in it without risk of sinking. As it dried out, it set hard like concrete and the only way to reach the buried treasures was to drill through the mud for them. By the time the workmen had fetched the right equipment from their base hundreds of kilometres away, the rains had fallen and refilled the lake.

Since then, the Colombian government has placed a ban on excavations on the lake and its long-held secrets are safe from prying eyes. A tantalizing glimpse of the amazing treasures which may still be hidden beneath the water was, however, discovered in 1969 by two farmers exploring a cave near the lake. They found a breath-takingly beautiful golden statue, of a man in a elaborate head-dress, standing on a golden raft and accompanied by eight oarsmen. There was only one person it could be – El Dorado, the Golden Man himself . . .

WAS COLUMBUS THE FIRST TO DISCOVER AMERICA?

"In fourteen hundred and ninety–two, Columbus sailed the ocean blue. . ."

Cristobal Colon (better known as Christopher Columbus) was born in Genoa, Italy, in 1451. Genoa was a busy port, and, from an early age Columbus was fascinated by ships and the sea. He learned navigation and chart-making and sailed on a number of expeditions. These were exciting times – the world was opening up for exploration and trade – and Columbus wanted to be part of them. His interest soon grew into an obsession and he became increasingly intrigued by the possibility of making the greatest voyage so far – across the Atlantic Ocean to the legendary lands of Cipangu (Japan) and Cathay (China), described by the explorer, Marco Polo. No one at that time had any idea of the size of the oceans nor of the existence, between Europe and the mystical East, of the great continents of North and South America. To fund such an ambitious expedition, however, Columbus first needed to find a sponsor who would back him.

The obvious person for Columbus to approach was the King of Portugal. Since the days of Prince Henry the Navigator in the early fifteenth century, Portuguese sailors had led the way in world exploration, particularly around Africa, and Columbus had already sailed in a Portuguese ship on an earlier expedition. But when Columbus presented his case to the Portuguese court, the king laughed in his face and refused to have any part in his madcap scheme. In France and England he met with the same response. Finally he turned to Spain. King Ferdinand and Queen Isabella agreed to put up the funds for an expedition of three ships – including Columbus's flagship, the *Santa Maria* – and one hundred and twenty men.

Columbus set sail in August 1492. His first stop was the Canary Islands where the expedition took on supplies of food and water. He then sailed west for thirty three days, without sighting land. Various mishaps and misfortunes overtook the expedition on its way. They were almost marooned in the Sargasso Sea when the ships became entangled in the thick, clogging mats of seaweed which cover the surface of the water. At other times, the sailors' spirits sunk so low that Columbus was forced to lie and tell them that they were not as far from home as they thought they were. At last, after many long days at sea, they reached land – the Bahamas. From there, they went to Cuba and the island of Hispaniola (now divided into the Dominican Republic and Haiti). To his dying day, Columbus was convinced that he had reached the unexplored shores of Cathay (China) and not the West Indies. Whilst on Cuba, he even sent out a mission to take greetings to Kublai Khan, the great Mogul leader. And, despite further expeditions

to the North American mainland and to the interior of South America, nothing could persuade him that he was wrong. He refused to accept that what he had discovered was a new continent. His crew had to swear on their lives that they agreed with him. If they broke their oaths, they ran the risk of having their tongues cut out.

So, Christopher Columbus was given the credit for being the first outsider to discover

America. But was he? A great many books have been written and theories put forward suggestions that explorers had already reached America long before Columbus sailed there in 1492. These are some of the main contenders:

2640 BC Two Chinese explorers, Hsi and Ho, may have reached America through the Bering Strait and sailed down the south coast as far as Guatemala.

First century BC Various Indian expeditions are said to have sailed across the Pacific to South America.

First century BC Expeditions from Egypt, Carthage and Phoenicia may also have reached America during this time. An American scientist points to the large number of Egyptian words used in various North American Indian languages as proof that the Egyptians did reach and explore the continent.

AD 550 An Irish monk, St Brendan, may have sailed from Ireland to Newfoundland in Canada in a curragh (a small boat built of wood and animal hides), with a group of 17 fellow monks. In 1977, the modern-day explorer, Tim Severin, followed in St Brendan's footsteps, making the same voyage in a reconstructed curragh.

9th-11th centuries The Vikings sailed westwards, discovering and colonising Iceland and

Greenland. An expedition led by Leif Erikson may have reached America in the early 11th century. The Vikings called the region, Vinland, because of all the grapevines that grew there. Most historians now agree that the Vikings did reach America before Columbus and the remains of a Viking campsite was recently discovered in Newfoundland. But there is little hard evidence apart from this. Could the Vikings really have sailed all that way in their wooden longships? According to the ancient Viking sagas (legends), the ships were indeed strong and sturdy enough to make such a voyage. The sagas also describe a landscape which matches that of Newfoundland and customs known to be those of the local Indian peoples. Besides, the Vikings had already reached Greenland, not that far away, and they were famous for their spirit of adventure.

12th century A Welsh prince, Madog An Owain Gwyneed, may have made two journeys to America.

14th century Abubakari, the Arab king of Mali, is reported to have sailed from Africa to Peru in South America.

1446 Explorers from Denmark and Portugal may have reached North America in their search for a trade route to Asia.

What do you think?

WHAT WAS FOUND IN THE MYSTERIOUS MONEY PIT?

On a tiny island in Mahone Bay, Nova Scotia, off the east coast of Canada, lies hidden one of the oddest and most intriguing mysteries of all. At the eastern end of Oak Island a deep natural shaft seemed to reach down to a large cavern some seventy metres below the surface. The shaft had been blocked by a system of wooden platforms. It had also been flooded through a series of tunnels leading off the main shaft. If anyone tried to reach the lowest level, they would cause the shaft to flood with seawater, unless they could find a way of damming up the side tunnels first. Whoever had constructed the mysterious "money pit" had gone to great and ingenious lengths to make sure that its secret contents never came to light. For rumour had it that a great store of treasure was buried in the pit. The island had certainly gained a reputation as a haven for pirates in the seventeenth and eighteenth centuries. Some people even linked the treasure to the notorious Captain Kidd. Could the money pit really contain a fabulous hoard of priceless pirate gold? For two hundred years, hopeful treasure-hunters have tried to find out . . .

The strange story of the money pit begins one day in 1795. Three local boys, Daniel McGinnis, aged 16, and two friends, were exploring Oak Island. In a small clearing, they came across an old, gnarled oak tree from which hung a heavy block and tackle (an old-fashioned device used for lifting heavy objects). On the ground beneath the block and tackle, they saw a slight, circular dip. The boys' excitement grew. From early childhood they had heard tales about cut-throat pirates and their stolen gold. Now Daniel was convinced that they had stumbled upon a buried treasure trove. The block and tackle were an enormous clue. Someone had obviously been here before and had used the block and tackle to lower a heavy load into the ground. The boys returned home for shovels and picks, and without further ado began to dig. Soon they realized that they were in a steep shaft, which still bore pick marks on its walls. A bit further down, they uncovered and removed a flagstone floor. Further down still, they came across two wooden platforms made of oak logs. But, without better tools and more help, they realized that this was as far as they could go. They went back to the mainland, vowing to return and continue their search.

Nine years later, in 1814, they went back to Oak Island to start work again on the mysterious money pit. They had persuaded a wealthy local business man to finance a full-scale operation to search the pit, in return for a share of the treasure, if and when they found it. A local workforce was recruited and the excavation began in earnest. As the shaft was sunk deeper, they found further oak platforms, sealed with putty and coconut fibre. At twenty eight metres down, they stumbled on an unsual stone, with a inscription written in secret code engraved on it. They wedged the stone out and took it home. The message, which was later decoded for them, read:

> *"Forty feet below, two
> million pounds are buried."*

Another wooden platform lay beneath the stone. Convinced that it covered a priceless treasure chest, they kept on digging, despite the fact that water began to pour in as they went deeper. The following day was Sunday and work was suspended while the men went to church. When they returned to the site on Monday, the shaft was completely flooded with water. Work, and treasure, were abandoned.

The mystery deepened in 1849, when anoth-

er group of wealthy businessmen banded together to make a further attempt on the pit. They included the youngest of the pit's original discoverers, now in his sixties. The original shaft had by now caved in and had to be redug to a depth of about twenty six metres.

All seemed well and the shaft was still dry. Yet again, work was halted on Saturday night and the men went to church on Sunday morning. When they returned to the site on Sunday afternoon, the shaft had flooded again. They were back to square one. After trying to bail the water out in buckets and to pump it out, they turned to a horse-driven drill called an auger which bored into the ground and brought up samples of the soil it drilled through. Five holes were drilled. The first two holes brought up only mud and stones. But the next two brought up fragments of oak and metal. In the minds of the diggers, there was only one object they could have come from – a treasure chest. As the fifth and final hole was sunk, commotion broke out among the drillers. The drilling foreman, a man called James Pitblado, was accused of taking something shiny from the bore sample and of putting it in his pocket. Pitblado refused to show them what the mysterious object was. He later tried to buy Oak Island but the owners refused to sell. Local legend says that he found a precious jewel but he died soon afterwards, and his secret went with him to the grave. In 1850, the drilling expedition sank a new shaft. Once again, just as they thought they were about to reach the treasure chest at last, the sea flowed in.

Over the next few years, many expeditions tried, and failed, to find the Oak Island treasure. Attempts were made to drain the pit by sinking more shafts alongside the original one. But whoever had built the pit had been a highly skilled engineer. Then the excavators found the source of the water on a nearby beach, reached by a complex series of drains. At high tide, water poured along the drains and into the shaft. Every attempt ended in failure, as the new shafts flooded, too, and soon the eastern end of the island was completely churned to mud by tunnels, shafts and excavations. In 1970, a salvage company launched the biggest, and costliest, onslaught to date on the mysterious money pit. Using the latest equipment, the company dug deeper into the shaft than any previous excavators and revealed the existence of a cave, or cavern, at the bottom of the shaft. Underwater cameras also sent back pictures of piles of old logs on the cave floor, and, so the rumours said, three treasure chests and a human hand which had been chopped off at the wrist.

But who built the pit and what exactly is buried there? These questions remain unanswered to this day. One theory names Captain William Kidd, the famous pirate, as the most likely candidate. On the day before he was hanged (the fate awaiting all pirates if they were caught), he is said to have offered to disclose the whereabouts of his buried treasure, valued at £100,000, if his life was spared. But the deal was presumably rejected, for Kidd was duly hanged and his tarred and feathered body hung on a spike as a warning to others not to follow in his footsteps. Kidd did leave behind him several clues, however, to the whereabouts of his buried treasure. The most important were four maps found inside some old chests which may have belonged to Kidd himself. Experts say that the writing on the maps matches Captain Kidd's handwriting. Could the maps show where Kidd buried his fabulous store of treasure? And could the treasure island shown on the map be Oak Island?

CHAPTER 3
STRANGE CREATURES

DO YETIS EXIST?

Ever since people began to explore the remote reaches of Nepal and Tibet, they have brought back hair-raising tales of a huge and mysterious beast, half-man, half-ape, which lives among the mountains of the mighty Himalayas – the infamous Yeti, or abominable snowman. It is not only in the Himalayas that these shy, shambling creatures have been sighted. Elsewhere in Asia, they are known as Metis, Shookpas and Kang-Mis. In Russia, they are called Almas. To people living in the vast coniferous forests of northwest America, the creature is called Bigfoot while, in the Canadian Rockies, stories are told of the mysterious Sasquatch. However much the name varies from place to place, the descriptions of the creature itself are remarkable in their similarities - a creature over 3 metres tall, heavily built and hairy like an ape but which walks upright on two legs. Its species is unknown. So, are there Yetis living among the snow-capped peaks of the world's highest mountains? Or are they simply a figment of an exhausted explorer's imagination. After all, in the thin air of the mountains, it is all too easy to think you are seeing things . . .

The earliest account of Yetis to reach the West appeared in 1832, when a British official in Nepal, B.H. Hodson, described a bizarre creature the like of which he had never seen before, which had been terrorizing a group of local mountain porters. According to Hodson, the creature "moved erectly, was covered in long, dark hair and had no tail". He had no idea what it was. In 1889, another British official, Major L.A. Waddell, was out exploring some 6,000 metres up in the Himalayas when he came across a series of huge footprints in the snow, bigger than anything made by human feet. The team of local porters travelling with him told him that the tracks were made by a Yeti, a fierce creature known to attack and eat human beings. According to local legend, the best way to escape from a Yeti was to run away downhill, for as the Yeti ran after you, its long hair would fall in its eyes and blind it.

Further sightings followed in the years to come, of dark, upright creatures shambling across the snow and shadows high up on the mountain slopes. At first, scientists dismissed them as sheer fantasy or as cases of mistaken identity but, in most of the stories, there was a grain of truth, just about large enough to give even the most hard-bitten cynics a moment of doubt. Then, in 1951, came the sensational publication of a series of photographs which caused that doubt to grow and thrust the Yeti firmly back into the limelight.

The photographs were taken by Eric Shipton, a British mountaineer, who was part of an expedition to climb Everest, the world's highest mountain. As he was crossing the Menlung Glacier on Everest, he saw a line of enormous footprints. They were too large to have been made by a bear. They were also very fresh. "What really made my flesh creep," Shipton said later, "was that where we had to jump over crevasses, you could clearly see where the creature had dug its toes in." He photographed the footprints, standing an ice axe next to them to give the outside world an idea of scale. The footprints were 45 centimetres long and over 30 centimetres wide, with one huge, round toe and three smaller toes. The only creature known to make even a vaguely similar footprint was an orang-utan. But orang-utans live thousands of kilometres away on the island of Borneo and their big toes are longer than the toes in the mysterious prints.

Shipton had no possible reason for making his story up or for faking the photographs. But they were still not authentic enough to convince some hard-bitten scientists of the Yeti's existence. A leading authority at the British Museum claimed that the footprints must have been made by a type of ape, called a Himalayan langur. He backed up his claim with a description of the Yeti by Sherpa Tensing, one of the first men to reach the summit of Mount Everest. Tensing described the Yeti as having reddish-brown fur and being about 1.5 metres tall. This fitted in well with the appearance of a langur. But the theory was otherwise so full of flaws that most other scientists simply laughed at it. The identity of the Yeti remained a mystery.

Following Shipton's photographs, the craze for Yeti-hunting grew and grew. Still no one managed to catch a Yeti but the number of sightings and clues continued to increase year by year. One man claimed to have been badly mauled by a Yeti in Sikkim (a tiny kingdom in the Himalayas). Part of a hand, said to belong to a Yeti, was found in Nepal. In 1954, the *Daily Mail*, a London newspaper, sponsored an expedition to try and capture a Yeti at last. For almost four months, the members of the expedition traipsed over the snowy mountain slopes, without seeing so much as the briefest glimpse of the mysterious and elusive creature. They did, however, find some more footprints and some droppings, which were thought to be those of a Yeti.

But the expedition's most exciting find was the discovery of a number of Yeti "scalps", kept in some of the ancient Buddhist monasteries nestling among the mountains, which the monks worshipped as sacred relics. The expedition managed to track down several of these amazing scalps which were long and cone-shaped, with a crest of hair running down the middle. Some of the scalps were obvious fakes – made from assorted pieces of animal skin and hair sewn together. But some looked more convincing and when experts analysed the hair, they announced that it came from an animal so far unkown to science. Could this, at last, be the breakthrough dreamt of for so many years by generations of Yeti-hunters? Unfortunately, not. One of the scalps was taken back to Europe for further expert analysis. This revealed that the hair and skin came from a type of goat, called a serow, which lives in Nepal. The scalp did not belong to a Yeti. It was not, however, a deliberate fake nor an attempt to mislead scientists. Such scalps had been used in religious ceremonies for centuries, and had, along the way, been given the name of "Yeti scalps" because this is genuinely what people believed them to be.

And so the search for the Yeti continued . . .

There are various theories about what type of creature the Yeti could turn out to be. One suggestion is that it is a descendant of Gigantopithecus, a giant prehistoric ape which lived about 500,000 years ago. From various remains, including some ancient teeth found in a Chinese medicine shop, this ape was about twice the height of a modern-day gorilla and so would have stood about four metres tall. It was argued that these giant apes may have been pushed out of their forest homes because they could not compete for survival with human beings and that they may have moved to the safety and isolation of the mountain regions to avoid being completely wiped out. It is just possible that their descendants may have survived there ever since.

Another popular theory links the Yeti with Neanderthal Man, one of the ancestors of modern human beings who lived mainly in Europe some 70,000 to 35,000 years ago. Neanderthal Man was smaller than modern man, hairier and more ape-like in appearance. About 35,000 years ago, Neanderthal Man vanished from the face of the Earth, to be replaced by Cro-Magnon Man, our direct ancestor. The facts surrounding his disappearance remain a mystery. One suggestion is that he, like the giant prehistoric ape above, was pushed into the wilder, more remote regions of the Earth in order to survive. Were these ancient wild men the ancestors of the Yeti?

Adding to the mystery of the Yeti are the numerous sightings of similar creatures in the forests of Canada (Sasquatch) and north-west America (Bigfoot). Hundreds of sightings have been reported and Yeti-like creatures have been blamed for a variety of crimes and other incidents, including hurling rocks at a miners' hut and tearing the heads off two gold prospectors. One man claimed to have been picked up by a Sasquatch as he lay in his sleeping bag at his campsite and taken back to its family cave. He fired his rifle at the creatures and made his getaway. A Canadian publishing company even offered a large reward to anyone who could bring in a Sasquatch (the name means "wild man of the woods" in a local Indian language) alive. The reward was never claimed . . .

In 1967, another crucial piece of evidence emerged about the existence of the Yeti. On 20 October, a rancher, Roger Patterson, was riding through Bluff Creek in northern California when his horse suddenly bolted and he was thrown from the saddle. When he got to his feet and looked around, he could not believe his eyes. Some way in front of him, across the creek, was a tall, hairy creature that walked upright like a

person. Thinking quickly, Patterson grabbed his cine-camera and started filming the extraordinary beast. The creature stopped in its tracks, looked around at him, then began to run away. He followed the creature for some way through the woods but soon lost track of it. Patterson's film became famous throughout the world. It shows a rather blurred picture of a creature over two metres tall, with reddish-brown hair and large furry breasts. As it strides past Patterson, swinging its arms, it turns and looks straight into the camera. Was it the legendary Bigfoot that Patterson saw? Or was the film a clever hoax? Some scientists dismissed it as a fake –

the creature was obviously a man dressed up in a monkey suit, they said. Others were not so sure. After all, the film, and Patterson himself, seemed genuine enough . . .

And so the mystery of the Yeti remains. Until someone, some day, somewhere, captures a Yeti and scientists can study it properly, its existence cannot be proved beyond doubt. There is certainly plenty of evidence in favour of Yetis. Moreover, there have been hundreds upon hundreds of sightings of Yetis and similar creatures. Can they *all* be wrong?

IS THERE A MONSTER IN LOCH NESS?

On a dull, cloudy day, when the vast reaches of Loch Ness stretch out murky, grey and sinister before you, it is easy to believe that a monster of some sort lurks in the depths of the lake. For the lake is the largest in Britain, so deep at its greatest depth that it could swallow up most of the world's tallest buildings. It is more than 300 million years old, a huge crack in the Earth's surface which opened up as as result of an ancient earthquake. Today, you can drive round the lake on fast, modern roads but this was not always the case. Until the eighteenth century, the loch was practically unreachable, except by remote, winding trackways. For thousands and even millions of years, therefore, a monster may have been hiding in the lake's mysterious waters, completely unnoticed . . .

The earliest printed reports of a monster in Loch Ness appeared in about AD 565 when the mysterious beast is said to have been sighted by an Irish monk, St Columba. This first account appears in a book about the saint's life by his biographer, St Adamnan, writing about a century after his death. The story goes that one day St Columba arrived at the lake shore to board the ferry across. The ferry was nowhere to be seen so one of Columba's disciples volunteered to swim across the mile-wide lake to fetch a boat from the opposite shore for his master to cross in. As he swam, a terrible monster "something like a frog, only it was not a frog" suddenly rose to the surface of the lake "with a great roar and an open mouth". Everyone who saw the hideous monster was "stricken with very great terror". But St Columba is said to have averted the danger by making the sign of the cross and, with the words, "Go no further, nor touch that man. Quick, go back. . .", commanding the monster to go away. And, it is reported, at these words, the mighty beast meekly turned tail and fled.

Since then, there have been hundreds of other sightings, descriptions of the Loch Ness monster, photographs and theories about what type of beast it could be. Here are a few of the most important dates in monster-hunting history:

1871
A Scottish doctor reports seeing a monster which looks like an upturned boat but moves very quickly "wriggling and churning up the water".

1930
Three young men out fishing on the loch hear a loud splashing and see a large creature swimming towards them underwater. They are convinced that it is a monster and "certainly not a basking shark or a seal".

1933
A couple from London are driving along the loch side on their way back home after a holiday in Scotland. It is about four o'clock in the afternoon. About 200 metres ahead of them, they see a long, dark shape stretched across

the road. As they get nearer, they realize what it is – a long, grey neck, followed by a thick, grey body about 1.5 metres tall. It is moving across the road towards the lake in a series of jerky movements and seems to be carrying something in its mouth. "It was horrible," Mr Spicer later says of the beast. "An abomination." He also describes it as looking like "a huge snail with a long neck". But what is it? At the time the road is being newly built and there are frequent explosions as the workmen blast through the rock to clear a path. Could the noise have disturbed the monster from the

depths of the loch? Is the object in its mouth a dead sheep? Whatever it is and whatever it is carrying, the legend of Nessie is born.

1933

A vintage year for sightings of the monster. Another visitor, Miss N. Simpson sees the monster lying motionless in the water. It stays there for about ten minutes, then speeds away faster than a motor boat. A director of London Zoo dismisses the wealth of sightings as "a striking example of mass hallucination".

1934

A Benedictine monk from an abbey on the lake shore is working in the boathouse when he realizes that he is being watched — by the monster. He describes it as having a long, graceful neck with a white stripe down the front and a muzzle like a seal's muzzle.

1938

One eyewitness report claims that the monster has two humps. Another puts the number of humps at seven!

1959

The first scientific exploration of Loch Ness sets out, equipped with a variety of cameras and an echo-sounder for probing the lake's deep, dark secrets. The echo-sounder tracks a large, humped object as it dives and finds enough fish to feed several monsters, not just one. Today, you can hire your very own monster-hunting boats from the lake shore, complete with echo-sounding equipment!

1961

A registered charity, the Bureau for Investigating the Loch Ness Phenomena, is set up to do precisely what its name suggests. Several sightings are made by the Bureau. Its founder, the naturalist, Sir Peter Scott, concludes that "There are probably about twenty to fifty of them down there. I think they are related to plesiosaurs."

1969

A man called Frank Searle from London gives up his job to camp full-time by Loch Ness and watch for the monster. In 1971, he finally sees it. It is "seven feet long, dark and knobbly on top, smooth dirty white underneath". He remains by the lake for four years, photographing and recording the monster's movements. His tent quickly beccomes a tourist attraction in its own right. In June 1974, he has his most sensational sighting yet. This is his own account of what he saw, ". . . *two of the strangest little creatures I've ever seen. They were about two feet in length, dark grey in colour, something like the skin of an elephant, small heads with black protruding eyes, long necks and plump bodies. They had snake-like tails wrapped along their sides, and on each side of the body, two stump-like appendages*". As he creeps closer, the two extraordinary creatures scuttle off into the water. The Canadian tourists with him back up his sighting. But his photographs are not so reliable — it is proved that they have been tampered with, even to the extent of adding an extra hump to the monster!

1971

A local woman, Margaret Cameron, describes the monster like this, "It had a huge body and its movement as it came out of the trees was like a caterpillar." She sees the monster some time during World War I.

1975

A team of American scientists launch an expedition to find the monster. They use sophisticated underwater cameras and a "cocktail" of essence of sea cows, eel and sealion to attract Nessie towards the camera. They don't find anything but that doesn't stop them expressing their firmly-held belief in the monster's existence.

1987

An expedition named "Operation Deepscan" spends a week patrolling the loch, searching for evidence with a flotilla of twenty four launches equipped with sonar. The expedition costs a staggering £1,000,000. Although the sonar does record a large, moving object in the depths of the loch, the expedition leaves Loch Ness with the mystery still unresolved.

So, if Nessie does exist, what about the evidence? The first photograph of the monster was taken in November 1933 by a visitor to the loch, Hugh Gray. But he was so afraid of being ridiculed for claiming to have seen the monster that he left the film in his camera for several weeks, leaving himself open to further criticism. The photograph was published in the London *Daily Sketch* and the Scottish *Daily Record*. It shows a dark shadow with the vague outline of a bulky grey creature rising from the water. An expert zoologist from Glasgow University dismissed it scornfully. It was not like any living thing he'd ever seen, he said. But the most famous photograph of the monster appeared the following year, in April 1934. It became known as the "surgeon's photograph" because it had been taken by a London surgeon, Robert Wilson, as he was driving past the loch with a friend on his way to a bird-watching holiday. It was early in the morning and he stopped his car and got out to get a good view of the loch. Suddenly, the two men noticed a commotion on the surface of the water. What was happening? Then they saw it. Wilson rushed back to the car, grabbed his camera and began to snap frantically away. In his excitement, he had the photographs developed that very same day. Several were blank. But one was superbly clear. It showed a long, neck with a tiny head, arched over the water. The photograph was printed in the *Daily Mail* on 21 April 1934. It caused a sensation. Of course, opinions were divided about its authenticity. Many scientists dismissed it as fake. Some claimed that the photo showed a mass of rotting plants and weeds or the tip of a diving otter's tail. But many other people were convinced that this was the real thing.

Further photographs and even short films of the monster followed. In 1951, a local forestry worker, Lachlan Stuart, who lived beside the loch, was milking his cows early one morning when he noticed something racing across the loch. At first he thought it must be a speedboat, but then he noticed three humps on its back. He rushed to fetch his camera, and a family friend to witness the event, and snapped the monster as it sped towards the shore. Stuart only managed to take one photograph before his camera jammed, but he was sure that what he had seen was indeed the monster. Other people were not so certain. Many experts continued to dismiss the photos and films as being pictures of seals, large fish, otters or simple tricks of the light. The first moving pictures thought to be of Nessie were taken in 1960 by an engineer, Tim Dinsdale. He had such great faith in his film that he gave up his job to live in a small boat on the loch – another full-time monster hunter.

So, does the monster actually exist? Or is it an elaborate hoax thought up by the Scottish Tourist Board to attract visitors to the region? It has certainly proved a monster money spinner. But this suggestion doesn't explain the fact that a great many people claim to have seen the monster, among them monks, scientists, school teachers and others who are unlikely to be making the whole thing up. If the monster does exist, what sort of creature is it? One theory is that it must be related to plesiosaurs, prehistoric fish-eating sea reptiles with the long, snake-like neck and small head characteristic of many descriptions of Nessie. These creatures had, officially, been extinct for 70 million years. Could an isolated family have survived for all that time in the murky depths of the loch? The monster-hunter, Ted Holiday, suggested that the monster might be a giant version of the common slug. Slugs are related to squid and octopus which gave rise to many ancient legends about dragons and sea-serpents.

Whatever sort of creature it is that we are dealing with, the fact remains that Loch Ness is not the only lake where monsters are said to live. Similar beasts have been sighted in lakes not only in Scotland but all over the world – in Europe, China, Africa, Australia, Japan, South East Asia and so on and so on. Here is just a very small selection of them:

· **Gairloch, Scotland**
Monster: <u>unnamed</u>
Description: "A terrible beast as big as greyhound, that struck down great trees and slew three men with three strokes of its tail".

- Lake Morar, Scotland.

Monster: Mhorag.

Description: about the size of an Indian elephant, with four humps and a snake-like head.

- Lake Okanangan, Canada.

Monster: Ogopogo.

Description: a long-necked creature very like Nessie. Eats live sheep and cattle.

- Lake Champlain, USA

Monster: "Champ"

Description: "As thick as a man's thigh, with silver-grey scales that a dagger couldn't pierce and two-and-a-half foot jaws filled with lethal teeth". Local people claimed that the monster had magic teeth which can cure many types of illness and disease. Sceptics claim the monster is actually just a very large fish called a sturgeon.

- Lough Nahooin, Ireland

Monster: unnamed

Description: eel-like with two humps, a flat tail and horns on its head.

FOOTPRINTS OF THE DEVIL?

England. Winter 1855. The country lies in the grip of one of the coldest, iciest winters anyone can remember. Even in the south-western part of the country, which usually escapes the worst of the weather, the ground is covered in a thick blanket of snow. . .

Topsham, Devon. 8 February. Albert Brailsford, headmaster of the village school, opens his front door and shivers. It has snowed again in the night and the morning is bitterly cold. He sighs and shuts the door behind him, then sets off on his short walk to work . . .

As he walked down the village street, Albert Brailsford was puzzled by a line of strange prints in the snow. At first, they looked like footprints; on closer inspection, they seemed more likely to be hoofprints. They were shaped like small horseshoes, each one about ten centimetres long. Surely they must have been made by a horse. But, thought Albert Brailsford, this was no ordinary horse. For the hoofprints ran in a dead straight line, one in front of the other. To make prints like these, a horse would have had to have hopped down the street on one leg! Besides, the prints were only about twenty centimetres apart, and each one was crystal clear as if it had been branded or carved into the snow.

Albert followed the prints down the street, pointing them out to various friends and acquaintances as he went. Soon, a small crowd had tagged along with him, all agreeing that the prints belonged to no animal that they had ever seen before. They followed the trail southwards through the snow, until it came to a halt by a high brick wall. The villagers were baffled. Minutes later, they were more baffled still . . . for the tracks continued on the other side of the wall, in the same straight line as before. But how had the creature got over the wall? The snow on top of the wall showed no signs of disturbance. Had the creature cleared the wall with one great leap? Or had it walked straight through it? The mystery was growing deeper by the minute?

The villagers followed the prints to a haystack. They stopped on one side, then continued on the other, yet the haystack looked completely undisturbed. They passed under bushes, stopped at one end of a drainpipe and began again at the other end, they even went over rooftops. Sometimes they went up to the front doors of houses, then seemed to change their mind and double back on themselves again. They continued for many kilometres along the Devon coast, always in a straight line. Were they the work of a practical joker? Or were they more sinister than than? The practical joker theory was quickly dismissed. After all, whoever it was would not only have to have worn horseshoes attached to his shoes but would also have had to leap over walls, vault over haystacks and clamber over rooftops. He would also have had to cover long distances through deep snow and appalling weather.

The villagers had another theory . . . Some of the hoofprints had a split in the middle, as if they had been made by a cloven hoof. And, as far as the villagers knew, the only creature with cloven hooves was the Devil himself. These must be the Devil's footprints! From now on, everyone in the village was on their guard. Little old ladies locked their doors; men armed with pitchforks and guns stood guard at night. Of course, there were many who laughed at the villagers and their fears. "How quaint," they sneered. The tracks must have been made by some sort of animal, simple as that. But even they had to admit that not all the pieces of the puzzle fitted their explanation.

On 16 February 1855, the story of the hoofprints appeared in the London *Times* newspaper. It added that the prints had been seen in most, if

not all, of the villagers' gardens. No one was spared. The next day, a report in the *Plymouth Gazette* suggested that the creature was a kangaroo (a theory put forward by a local clergyman). It would certainly have explained the leaping over walls but one glaring error remained – kangaroos do not have hooves. Another paper printed the (almost) equally implausible story that the prints must have been made by a bird but birds don't have hooves either.

Several more theories were proposed in the *London Illustrated News*. The famous naturalist, Sir Richard Owen, examined the tracks and announced that they must have been made by a badger, come out of hibernation to search for food. He did not, however, offer any explanation of why the badger seemed to have hopped from place to place on one leg! Other candidates included otters, great bustards, polecats, hares, even bouncing rats (producing horseshoe-shaped indentations as they landed)! There was even talk (though some time later) that the prints had been made by some kind of UFOs.

Perhaps the most plausible explanation was offered by the editor of a book about the hoofprints. He suggested some sort of experimental balloon had been accidentally released from the local dockyard. It had broken free of its moorings and dragged two shackles on the ends of ropes as it trailed over the countryside. The hoofprints could be none other than the impressions made by these shackles in the snow. It's certainly possible but it still leaves several questions outstanding, questions which can never now be answered. It's not the first time the Devil's footprints have been seen. And it may not be the last . . .

AMELIA EARHART'S FINAL FLIGHT?

The Daily Mystery

19 July 1937

News just in. Hopes of finding America's favourite airwoman faded today as the official search for Amelia Earhart and her co-pilot and navigator, Fred Noonan, was called off. The pair had been attempting to circumnavigate the globe around the Equator. Beginning in Miami, USA, their route had taken them to Puerto Rico, Venezuela, Brazil, Senegal, Suda, India, Singapore, Australia and New Guinea and on towards the Pacific and the homeward leg of the journey.

The last contact with Amelia Earhart was on 1 July when she radioed, "We are flying north-east". Nothing has been heard from her since. A full-scale search in the region south of Hawaii was ordered immediately by President Roosevelt. The search was concentrated around Howland Island, Phoenix Islands where an emergency landing could have been made, and the Gilbert Islands.

The Lockheed Electra plane in which Miss Earhart was flying had been carefully prepared for the journey, although mechanical failure has not been ruled out at this stage. A problem may have arisen with the plane's radio equipment – an antenna had been left behind in Miami. This may have led to a crucial breakdown in communications.

Her final radio message was picked up by a passing US Coastguard cutter, *Itasca*, at 8.43 a.m. on 1 July, an hour after she had reported that her plane only had enough fuel to last for another thirty minutes. Her plan had been to land the plane on Howland Island, some way south of Hawaii.

Chances of the pair surviving were rated by experts as extremely slim last night. If the airplane floated on landing in the ocean, Miss Earhart and Mr Noonan may have been able to drift to safety. But the waters in that region of the Pacific are notoriously shark-infested and there seems little hope of finding them alive in such a vast expanse of ocean.

Amelia Earhart leaves behind a husband, George Putnam. The couple were married on 7 February 1931. In her short life, she had, time and again, rewritten the history books of aviation, becoming the first woman to compete on an even keel with men for flying honours.

A brief outline of her remarkable career follows here:

• **16 May 1923** •

American pilot, Amelia Earhart became the first woman to receive an airplane pilot's certificate from the US National Aeronautic Association.

• 18 June 1928 •

Amelia Earhart today became the first woman to cross the Atlantic by air. She was one of a three-person crew who took off from Trepassey, Newfoundland at 2.51 p.m. (British time) yesterday, bound for Ireland. Miss Earhart, former holder of the world altitude record, had to be content this time with being a passenger in the Fokker F.VIIb-3m Friendship, flown by pilots "Slim" Gordon and Wilmer Stultz. Crammed in a seat between the fuel tanks, Miss Earhart kept a log of the entire journey, recording the rain, fog and darkness through which the airplane finally flew on its 24-hour, 49-minute flight. With fuel supplies running low, the airplane landed safely, not in Ireland, but in Wales.

• 8 June 1931 •

Disappointment awaited Amelia Earhart when she arrived in Los Angeles today, believing herself to be the first person to fly across the USA in an autogyro. In fact, this record had been claimed just a week earlier, by the New York pilot, Johnny Miller. Miss Earhart had, this time at least, been pipped at the post. Her flight had been delayed several weeks as she recovered from illness. She now plans to return to New York to prepare for her next record-breaking attempt. Miss Earhart's flight was sponsored by the makers of Beechnut chewing gum.

• 21 May 1932 •

Amelia Earhart landed near Londonderry, Northern Ireland today – the first woman to fly solo and non-stop across the Atlantic. The official time given for her crossing was 14 hours and 54 minutes, beating the previous record held by Alcock and Brown by more than an hour. Her achievement is all the more remarkable given the problems she encountered during the flight. Shortly after taking off from Newfoundland, Canada, the plane's altimeter, a vital piece of flying equipment, failed. Miss Earhart then flew into a thunderstorm. As she tried to climb above the clouds, the plane became covered in ice and went into a thousand-metre spin. But the last two hours of the flight were the most nerve-wracking of the whole journey. As fire broke out in one of the engines, fuel being to leak into the cockpit. The plane could have gone up in flames at any minute. This was also the longest non-stop flight by a woman.

• 25 August 1932 •

At 11.31 a.m., Amelia Earhart arrived in Newark, New Jersey to set three more records in her ever-increasing list. These included becoming the first woman to fly non-stop across the USA. She also set the woman's distance flying record and broke her own woman's coast-to-coast record time (set last month) by almost ten minutes. The new record stands at 19 hours and 5 minutes. However, she failed to beat the overall coast-to-coast record of 18 hours and 22 minutes, set by Frank Hawks.

• 12 Jan 1935 •

The record books continue to be rewritten. Today, the amazing Miss Amelia Earhart became the first woman to fly solo across the Pacific, at the controls of a Lockheed Vega. A huge crowd gathered in San Francisco to watch her land after an 18-hour flight from Honolulu, Hawaii. Throughout her flight, Miss Earhart gave regular broadcasts on radio stations along the length of the US Pacific coast. During one broadcast, listeners feared the worst as her voice faded and died out. Fears grew that she had collapsed at the controls. Happily, she was later to explain that she had just got tired of flying over seemingly endless banks of fog.

• 20 March 1937 •

Amelia Earhart's first attempt at flying round the world ended in disaster at dawn today when a tyre on her Lockheed Electra aircraft exploded during take-off. The airplane was badly damaged and the attempt abandoned. Fortunately, Miss Earhart herself and her two navigators escaped unharmed.

Amelia Earhart's body has never been found . . .

THE MYSTERY OF THE MARY CELESTE
The Ship that Sailed Itself

On the afternoon of 5 December 1872, a watchman on board the English ship, *Dei Gratia*, sighted a two-masted vessel which seemed to be sailing way off course in the North Atlantic, midway between the Azores and the Portuguese coast. The ship seemed to be sailing unsteadily and out of control, as if its crew were drunk. The captain of the *Dei Gratia*, unable to see anyone at the ship's helm, sent out a signal but there was no answer to it. He then ordered the *Dei Gratia* to sail closer to the mysterious ship, a task made difficult by the choppy, squally sea. As they closed in, a boat was lowered into the sea and three men, the captain among them, rowed towards the stricken ship. Soon they were near enough to read her name – the *Mary Celeste*.

The captain and his two companions clambered aboard the *Mary Celeste*. No one came forward to greet them and there was no sight or sound of life on deck. The mystery deepened as they searched the ship from top to bottom. The vessel was in excellent condition – her sails, masts and timbers were all sound; her cargo of barrels of alcohol was still tied in place in the hold; there was plenty of food and water on board. But the ship was completely deserted. Her crew was nowhere to be seen and she seemed to be sailing herself, across the Atlantic Ocean.

It looked as if the ship had been suddenly, and recently, abandoned. In the sailor's quarters below deck, the crew's clothes and belongings were all in place and in good condition. Stranger still, were the steel razors which had not yet rusted (metal rusts quickly in the salty sea air) – another clue that the ship had not been abandoned long. In the galley kitchen, a cooking pot hung over a now dead fire. It contained the remains of a meal which were still reasonably fresh. In the captain's cabin, the table was laid for breakfast, with a half-finished bowl of porridge and a half-eaten boiled egg. Someone had taken a spoonful of cough mixture and not had time to replace the cork in the medicine bottle. Everything else in the cabin was, as in the rest of the ship, in its proper place and undamaged. It was as though the captain and the whole crew had suddenly, and en masse, decided to abandon ship.

But why had they taken this sudden and mysterious decision? Where had they gone to after abandoning the ship? So began the mystery of the *Mary Celeste*, a mystery which is no nearer to being solved today than it was more than a century ago. By the time it was discovered, sailing itself across the Atlantic, the *Mary Celeste* had already had a chequered history. Many sailors said the boat was jinxed and refused to sail in her. Built in 1860, in Nova Scotia, she was originally named *Amazon* and was launched in 1861. Tragedy struck not long after when her captain fell ill and died. Further misfortune followed. On her maiden voyage, the *Amazon* ran into a fishing weir, badly damaging her hull and having to return to the shipyard for repairs. Her first crossing of the Atlantic went smoothly until she collided with another ship in the Straits of Dover. Once again, she went back to the shipyard for further repairs. When she sailed again, back to America, under the command of a new captain (her fourth), she ran aground off Cape Bay in Nova Scotia. After this, the *Amazon* seems to have changed owners several times, as each in turn suffered some sort of misfortune, such as bankruptcy. She was finally bought by a group of New York shipowners, J.H. Winchester and Co, repaired, refitted and renamed . . . as the *Mary Celeste*. If her short life as the *Amazon* was unlucky, her time as the *Mary Celeste* was an unmitigated disaster. But this was far from the minds of her captain and crew as, in the autumn of 1872, they prepared the ship to sail once more from New York, across the Atlantic to Genoa in Italy.

Her crew of ten – Captain Benjamin Briggs, his wife, their two-year-old daughter and seven crewmen – prepared to board the Mary Celeste. Meanwhile, the ship's cargo – 1700 barrels of alcohol – was loaded into the hold and firmly lashed in place. This was Captain Brigg's fourth command. He came from a seafaring family, one of four brothers who all went to sea. He was also a deeply religious man, described by those who knew him as "always bearing the highest character as a Christian and as an intelligent and active shipmaster". He also held shares in the *Mary Celeste*. The rest of the crew were all honest, upright, well-respected and experienced sailors – it looked set to be a pleasant, successful and uneventful voyage. On 7 November, delayed by several days of stormy weather, the *Mary Celeste* finally set sail. Its crew was never to be seen again.

The *Dei Gratia* set sail from New York eight days after the *Mary Celeste*. She was bound for Gibraltar with a cargo of petroleum. It was early afternoon on 5 December when they sighted the *Mary Celeste* and went aboard to investigate. Although they searched the ship thoroughly for more than an hour, the boarding party could find no clues as to why she had been so suddenly abandoned by the crew nor to the crew's whereabouts. Captain Brigg's last entry in the ship's log was made on 25 November. It read:

Monday, 25th. At five o'clock made island of St Mary's bearing ESE. At eight o'clock Eastern point bore SSW 13 kilometres (6 miles) distant.

In the mate's cabin they found a chart showing the course the ship had taken up to 24 November. The only things missing from the ship were the ship's chronometer, sextant, cargo documents, navigation book and a small boat that had been tied to the main deck. It was obvious that the *Mary Celeste*'s crew had abandoned ship. But why? The captain of the *Dei Gratia* suspected that there had been a mutiny on board. As evidence he pointed to a cutlass which appeared to be smeared with blood (though this was later disproved at the official enquiry). He also found similar stains on the deck rail. But there was something about the mutiny theory that didn't ring quite true . . .

A more immediate problem faced the captain – what to do with the *Mary Celeste* herself? According to international law, the *Dei Gratia's* captain was entitled to a share of the profits of any abandoned ship that he helped to salvage. Usually these vessels were wrecks and not worth a great deal. But the *Mary Celeste* was in first-class order, still seaworthy, with her cargo intact, and would fetch a substantial amount of money. Reluctantly – he did not really have the crew to spare – the captain agreed to send aboard a party of men to put the *Mary Celeste* in order and, two days later, both ships set sail for Gibraltar where they arrived on 12 and 13 December respectively. The *Mary Celeste* was immediately placed under arrest and an official investigation set in motion by the British Admiralty in Gibraltar.

The officer in charge of the investigation was an arrogant, self-centred man, Frederick Solly Flood. On the basis of the little evidence there was, he concluded that murder and mutiny were the only possible causes for the abandonment of the *Mary Celeste*. In his opinion, and this was the version of events accepted at various times by the British and American authorities, the crew had broken into the cargo of alcohol and, in a drunken frenzy, had murdered the captain and his family, then escaped on the missing boat. There were several flaws in his argument. Firstly, if the mutineers had escaped, surely at least some of them would have turned up again at a later date? Secondly, there were no signs of struggle on board (the bloodstains had been discounted by this time). Thirdly, the ship was carrying cargo of pure alcohol, more likely to make the drinker seriously ill before it made him drunk. The theory simply didn't stand up to closer examination and Flood was forced to back down.

His next theory was equally far-fetched. He suggested the Captain Briggs and the captain of the *Dei Gratia,* David Morehouse, were in it together and that Briggs had killed the crew, escaped in the boat and arranged to meet Morehouse some time later after Morehouse had claimed the salvage reward. But both captains were known to be men of good character and well-respected sailors with years of unblemished service behind them. No one seriously believed that either would be capable of such a deed. Following the same tangled thread of thought, Flood put forward yet another explanation. This time he accused Morehouse and his crew of boarding the *Mary Celeste* and murdering the crew themselves. By this time, the Admiralty Court had heard enough of Flood's theories. It cleared Captain Morehouse and the crew of the *Dei Gratia* of all charges and granted them their fair share of the salvage reward.

But the mystery surrounding the fate of the *Mary Celeste*'s crew would not go away. Hundreds of theories were put forward. Short stories and articles were written about the tragedy, many of which bore little resemblance to the facts. Books about the *Mary Celeste* became bestsellers on both sides of the Atlantic. People claiming to be survivors of the crew continued to come forward, though their names did not appear on the original crew list. The following are just some of the suggestions put forward over the years to explain the bizarre fate of the *Mary Celeste*:

• **Was the ship attacked by a huge, monstrous sea creature, such as a giant octopus or a sea serpent which plucked the crew from the ship and**

ate them? If so, how did it manage
to leave the ship undamaged and why
did it take the chronometer, sextant
and ship's paper with it?

· Was the ship swallowed up by another triangle, similar to the Bermuda Triangle?

· Were the ship and its crew abducted by a UFO?

· Were the supplies of food and water somehow contaminated with a substance which caused the crew to hallucinate, eventually driving them so mad that they flung themselves overboard?

· Was the ship put in danger by its cargo of alcohol? This was the theory put forward by one of its owners, James H. Winchester and various others. They suggested that the alcohol may have begun to give off potentially explosive fumes. Fearing that the Mary Celeste might blow up any minute, the crew abandoned ship in the small lifeboat. This was overloaded, capsized and the crew were drowned. This is what Oliver Cobb, Captain Briggs' nephew had to say about it:

"My theory is that Captain Briggs in the afternoon of November 24, 1872, fearing an explosion of the cargo of alcohol, put his wife and child in a boat with Mr Richardson (the first mate) and one sailor to care for them. Another sailor would hold the boat clear of the vessel. Mr Gilling (the second mate) with another sailor unrove the main-peak halliard as a towrope. The fourth sailor would be at the wheel. The captain went below and got the chronometer, sextant, and ship's papers. The cook was getting supplies to take in the boat. The cook evidently gathered up what food was available as no cooked food was found on the Mary Celeste. Probably at this time came a minor explosion which landed the hatch upside down on deck. They made haste to get away. . .The boat was hastily pushed away from the Mary Celeste."

• Was the Mary Celeste struck by a waterspout? This was the theory proposed by a former head of the United States Weather Bureau in New York. Although the damage caused by a waterspout may have been superficial and short–lived it may also have caused the ship's instruments to malfunction, leading the crew to believe that the ship was about to sink. The captain may have panicked and ordered the crew to abandon ship.

In 1913, some forty years after the event, another explanation was put forward. An article appeared in the *Strand* magazine in London, written by a schoolmaster, Howard Linford. A past employee, Abel Fosdyk, had left Linford some papers in his will. They told an extraordinary story . . .

Abel Fosdyk claimed that he had been a secret stowaway on board the *Mary Celeste*, on the ship's final, fateful voyage, and that he had been the only survivor. According to his papers, he had been a friend of Captain Briggs who, for some unknown reason (and seemingly out of character for such a god-fearing man), had given him safe passage when he had to leave America in a hurry. He said that, during the voyage, a special play-deck had been built for the captain's daughter. One day, Fosdyk said, the first mate challenged Captain Briggs to a swimming match, to see how well a fully-dressed man could swim. Briggs immediately took up the challenge, dived into the sea and began swimming a circuit of the ship. The first mate and another man followed.

Then disaster struck. As the first mate swam around the boat . . . he screamed and disappeared from sight. As the captain's wife, daughter and the remaining crew crowded on to the play-deck to see what had happened, the deck collapsed under their weight. According to Abel Fosdyk, they were thrown in the sea where they were attacked and eaten by sharks which had already accounted for the first mate. The only person to survive the disaster was Abel Fosdyk himself. He clung for his life to a piece of wreckage and was washed up, half-dead, some days later, on the northwest coast of Africa.

None of these theories fully explain all the aspects of the story – where the ship was found, the condition she was found in, why her crew abandoned her so suddenly but still found time to take certain things with them. Many get basic details about the ship and its crew completely wrong. No really satisfactory explanation has ever emerged. And it seems that, after more than a hundred years, the mystery of the *Mary Celeste* is no closer to being solved now than it was over a century ago.

SPONTANEOUS HUMAN COMBUSTION

Over the centuries, many bizarre and mysterious stories have come to light of people who, for no apparent reason whatsoever, suddenly and inexplicably burst into flames. But is spontaneous human combustion, as this phenomenon is known, mere superstition, magic or is there something more sinister to it than that? So far, no one has been able to come up with an even remotely believable explanation for this extraordinary phenomenon. It has baffled modern scientists and left the so-called experts admitting defeat or dismissing it as pure fantasy. Yet, cases are still being reported and many questions remain to be answered. . .

Case Study 1

One of the earliest cases of spontaneous human combustion was that of the 62-year-old Countess Cornelia Baudi from Verona who died in April 1731. Her body, or what remained of it, was discovered by her maid lying on the bedroom floor. Our knowledge of the case comes from the account of a young priest, a friend of the countess, who immediately wrote it all down.

The evening before had passed just as any other evening. The countess had retired to bed, chatted for a while with her maid, then had fallen into a deep sleep. In the morning, however, when the maid went back to the bedroom to wake her mistress, a terrifying sight awaited her. The air in the room was thick with acrid-smelling smoke. Soot covered every surface. The bed itself was undamaged. Indeed, the bed-covers had been thrown back as if the countess had just got out of bed, perhaps to open a window or fetch a drink of water. The maid screamed and ran to fetch the priest. This is what he saw:

"The floor of the chamber was

thickly smeared with a glue-like moisture, not easily got off and from the lower part of the window trickled down a greasy, loathsome, yellowish liquid with an unusual stink. Four feet from the bed was a heap of ashes, two legs untouched, stockings on, between which lay the head, the brain, half of the back part of the skull and the whole chin burned to ashes, among which were found three blackened fingers. All the rest were ashes which had this quality, that they left in the hand a greasy and stinking moisture . . ."

All that was left of the countess were her two stockinged legs, her half-burnt head and three charred fingers. The rest of her body had been engulfed by the flames.

Case Study 2

It was not until the nineteenth century that doctors and scientists would even admit that such a thing as spontaneous human combustion existed. Two cases, one in Britain and one in the USA, may have helped to change their minds.

In 1841, the *British Medical Journal*, a learned and respected publication, reported the death of a 40-year-old woman. She was found, her body still burning, lying on the floor near the hearth. Her legs had been burnt to a crisp, yet the stockings she was wearing had somehow escaped without any damage at all.

In 1880, in Massachusetts, USA, several people, including a respected local doctor, witnessed a woman suddenly burst into flames right before their eyes. The flames burst from her legs and chest and soon engulfed her whole body.

The phenomenon of spontaneous human combustion even gripped the imagination of several famous nineteenth century novelists, Charles Dickens among them. In Dickens' novel, *Bleak House*, the drunken rag-and-bone dealer, Mr Krook, spontaneously combusts after a bout of heavy drinking.

Case Study 3

In 1919, a writer, J. Temple Thurston, was found dead at his country home in Kent, England. He was found still sitting in his armchair, horribly burnt from the waist down. The rest of his body had not been touched by the flames, and, once again, his clothes showed no signs of damage. Incredibly, his lower body had burned away beneath his clothes without even scorching the material they were made from.

Case Study 4

The most famous recent case of spontaneous human combustion is that of Mrs Mary Reeser, an elderly woman aged 67, who lived in Florida, USA. On the evening of Sunday 1 July 1951, she was sitting in her armchair, smoking a cigarette. As usual, her landlady called in to say goodnight. Everything seemed normal.

Early the following morning, the landlady was awakened by a strong smell of smoke. Thinking that it must be the water pump overheating, she went to the garage and turned it off. Then she went back to bed. She was woken a few hours later by a knock on the front door. A telegraph boy stood there with a telegram for Mrs Reeser. The landlady signed for it and took it up to Mrs Reeser's apartment. To her amazement and alarm, the door knob was hot — too hot to touch. She called two painters, working nearby to come and help her. They managed to turn the knob and open the door. . . A blast of fiercely hot air met them as the door opened, yet there were no signs of fire inside the room. Then they noticed a charred patch on the carpet where Mrs Reeser's armchair had stood – only a few odd springs now remained. There was even less to be found of Mrs Reeser. She had burned to death in a fire of such intensity that all that remained of her body were a few grisly fragments – part of her spine with a piece of her head attached; her skull shrunk by the heat to the size of an orange; her left foot still in its slipper. Next to her body lay a newspaper, completely untouched by the flames. Nothing else in the room had been caught by the fire – only the armchair in which Mrs Reeser had been sitting.

At an inquest into Mrs

Reeser's death, no scientific reason could be found for the fire. The forensic scientist who investigated the case commented, "I regard it as the most amazing thing I have ever seen. As I review it, the hairs on my neck bristle with vague fear. Were I living in the Middle Ages, I would mutter something about black magic."

Case Study 5

Early in the morning of 5 December 1966, Don Gosnell, a gas meter reader, set off on his rounds in the town of Coudersport, Pennsylvania, USA. One of his first calls was to the home of a retired family doctor, Dr John Bentley. Dr Bentley was a frail old man who had difficulty walking, so Gosnell was not suprised that his knock on the door was not answered immediately. Instead, he let himself in . . . and then the smell of smoke hit him.

Gosnell saw no sign of a fire, nor of the doctor. He went down into the basement where the meters were housed. There he noticed a small pile of ash on the floor. What he did not notice was a hole in the ceiling (to the bathroom above) through which the ash appeared to have fallen. He read the meter and then went to find the doctor who had still not answered his call. The old man's bedroom was smoky but no one was there. Then something led Gosnell to the bathroom. He opened the door . . . What he saw filled him with horror.

Dr Bentley's walking frame lay by a blackened hole in the floor. Beside the frame he saw the remains of the doctor's right leg, with a slipper still on its foot. Apart from the pile of ash in the basement, that was all that was left of Dr Bentley. At the inquest that followed, the coroner suggested that Dr Bentley had accidentally set

fire to himself whilst lighting
his pipe. But the doctor's pipe
was still in its place on his
bedside table . . .

As yet, there have been no acceptable explanations of why people should suddenly, and without warning, burst into flames. There have been various suggestions, however. Some people thought that ball lightning must be the cause of the fire but this was later rejected. Others suggested that the victims were all heavy drinkers, or heavy smokers, or both. Perhaps the alcohol in their bloodstreams caught fire as they lit a cigarette? But it seems unlikely.

In 1725, an innkeeper was cleared of murdering his wife when a surgeon managed to persuade the court that the woman had been a victim of spontaneous human combustion. The final verdict was that the innkeeper's wife had died by a "visitation from God", another possible explanation perhaps.

What about electrical faults? Or gas leaks? A more recent book suggests that spontaneous human combustion is a result of mind over matter by people who can actually generate high voltages of electricity in their bodies with their minds, becoming in effect human electric batteries. Another theory is that spontaneous human combustion may be linked to "ley lines" – some people believe these are lines of energy originating deep inside the Earth. Finally, there are some people who blame the phenomenon on poltergeists, or "fire-spooks".

Certain patterns have emerged from the various cases which have been documented. The victims tend to be old people or young people. There is no visible source of fire and the victim's body is almost totally destroyed by the flames. Burning is limited to the victims and the immediate area around them. Their clothing is often left untouched. But all attempts to find the cause of this phenomenon have proved unsuccessful, so far. The mystery of spontaneous human combustion looks set to continue for many years yet . . .

THE TURIN SHROUD — HOLY RELIC OR HOAX?

In the Chapel of the Dukes of Savoy, in Turin Cathedral, Italy, lies one of the holiest relics of Christianity — a piece of linen cloth about 4 metres long by a metre wide, bearing the faint imprint of a man. This is the Holy Shroud of Turin. Every thirty three years, the length of Christ's lifetime, the shroud is put on display and thousands of pilgrims flock to catch a glimpse of what they believe to be the actual features of Christ himself. Ever since the discovery of the shroud, it has provoked more argument and controversy than almost any other relic. But is it truly a holy relic at all? Or is it, as modern scientific methods have shown, an ingenious, medieval fake?

The pilgrims who come to gaze on the shroud believe that this is the very piece of cloth which covered Christ's body as he lay in his tomb after the crucifixion. The image of his body appears to have become imprinted on the cloth, some say miraculously, some say by an early technique which predates photography.

The origins of the shroud are veiled in mystery. According to one of the many legends which surround the shroud, it was taken from Christ's body by one of his disciples, then kept in hiding for several centuries during the first few centuries after Christ's death when the early Christians were still being persecuted for their beliefs. It later made its way to Constantinople in Turkey where it remained until the city fell in 1204. The shroud was rescued by Crusader knights and taken for safekeeping to Besançon Cathedral in France. In 1349, it narrowly escaped being destroyed in a fire which swept through the cathedral building and, in 1432, it was presented to the Dukes of Savoy. After being slightly damaged in another fire, the shroud finally reached its present home, in the cathedral of Turin, in 1578. And so a legend was born.

Serious scientific interest in the shroud began the late nineteenth century, when an Italian archaeologist, Secondo Pia, took the first photographs of the relic. To his amazement, the negatives of the photographic plates showed a much clearer, sharper image of the figure's face and body than appeared on the cloth. Was this, remarkable as it sounded, the first ever photographic record of Christ? A few years later, Dr Yves Delage, a distinguished member of the French Academy of Science, furthered the speculation and the controversy. He examined the shroud and the photographs in minute detail and came to the following conclusions. The image was that of a man whose wounds showed that he had indeed been crucified. He had also been beaten – his face was battered and bruised, his nose badly injured. Most of his body bore marks which showed that he had been savagely flogged with a gruesome, lead-studded whip. Most telling of all, however, were the small, blood-encrusted gashes in his hands and feet – were these the stigmata, the marks made by the nails which held the man on the cross?

As for Dr Delage himself, his own personal belief was that all the signs and clues gleaned from the shroud were indeed consistent with the treatment of Jesus which had led to his death. It was not until the late 1980s that his theory was finally disproved by thorough scientific analysis of the shroud and its mysterious image.

Various experts had already cast doubt on the shroud's true identity. An art historian, who specialized in forgeries, tried to prove that the shroud was a fake by showing that

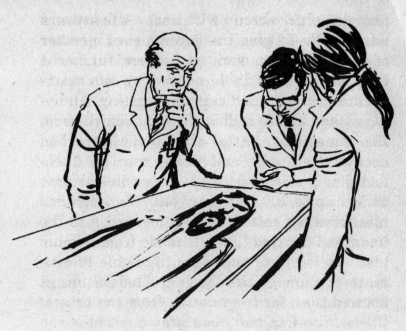

parts, at least, of the image had been painted on to the cloth. But, said his critics, these might have been added by later artists and the shroud might be genuine after all. However, even the firmest believers had to accept that the practice of painting on fine linen was widespread in the fourteenth century and that documentation from that time did exist which dismissed the shroud as having been "cunningly", and recently, painted.

In 1988, the Archbishop of Turin, in an attempt to solve the mystery once and for all, commissioned a team of scientists to test small samples of the shroud with a view to putting a date on it. To give the project even greater respectability, the work was supervised by the British Museum in London. The scientists used a method called carbon-14 dating. All living things absorb radioactive carbon rays from the atmosphere. After they die, the carbon decays at a known and steady rate. By calculating this rate of decay, it is possible to date things up to 100,000 years old. The scientists measured the rate at which the carbon in the linen had decayed (linen is made from a living plant called flax) and were thus able to estimate the age of the shroud. Their findings showed that, far from dating from the time of Christ, the flax had been grown sometime in the thirteenth or fourteenth century. This was about the time that a French nobleman first declared the shroud to be Christ's burial shroud. And about the time that it was dismissed as a fake, produced by a local painter, by the Bishop of Troyes, also in France.

However strong the scientific proof against the Holy Shroud of Turin, and it would seem to point, without a shadow of a doubt, to the fact that the cloth is a fake, many people remain unconvinced. To those who believe firmly in its sacredness, the shroud shows and always will show the face of Jesus Christ himself.

WHEN TIME SLIPS BY ...

Is it possible to travel backwards in time? The people involved in the following two incidents certainly believed so. One minute, they were living their own lives, in their own time, and the next they had slipped back in time to another world altogether.

• In 1901, two dons from Oxford University, Eleanor Jourdain and Charlotte Moberly, were visiting the Palace of Versailles near Paris. As they wandered through the beautiful palace gardens, they suddenly, and inexplicably, found themselves back in the Versailles of 1789, the year of the French Revolution, just before the downfall and execution of King Louis XVI and his wife, the infamous Marie Antoinette. Among the people they met were many who could talk of nothing else but the current political situation. Somehow, the two women had slipped back in time. Ten years later, they published an account of their experiences in a book entitled An Adventure. Their critics claimed that they must have stumbled upon a fancy dress party or an entertainment of some sort. But many people believed them. After all, why should they lie?

• In 1973, Jane O'Neill from Cambridge, England, was the first person to arrive at the scene of a particularly serious traffic accident involving a bus. She helped to free the injured passengers trapped inside. But the traumatic events she had witnessed left her in a state of shock. She had difficulty sleeping and, shortly after the accident, began to see things. On a visit to Fotheringay Church, her attention was caught by one particular picture, of the Crucifixion, hanging behind the church altar. Later, however, when she mentioned the picture to the friend who had been with her, the friend said she had seen no such thing. Further enquiries showed that the picture so admired by Mrs O'Neill had hung in the church in the 1500s, before the original building had been demolished in 1553. To have seen it, she must have slipped back several hundred years in time.

No reason has ever been found to disbelieve the narrators of these two stories. Why should otherwise perfectly respectable people bother to make up such outlandish tales? But if we do believe them, then we must also believe in time travel and it remains to be seen if we are quite ready for that!

WHO WAS KASPAR HAUSAR?

In the afternoon of 26 May 1828, a strange boy, aged about 16 years old, stumbled into the Unschlitt Square in the German city of Nuremberg. It was Whit Monday and the townspeople were enjoying a day's holiday. The boy stood out from the smartly dressed crowd – he was wearing a shabby coat with tattered trousers and a pair of battered, worn-out old boots. He staggered across the square, muttering and whimpering to himself. Most people who saw him thought he must be drunk, or mad, or both.

A local shoemaker, George Weichmann, felt sorry for the boy and hushed the taunts of the people around him.

"Now, young man, what's your name?" he asked gently. But the boy only carried on with his mumblings. He seemed not to know who he was, where he was or what was going on around him. It was as though he didn't even understand a word of what was being said to him. But he did manage to push a grubby-looking envelope into the shoemaker's hands. The letter it contained was addressed to:

"The Captain of the Fourth Squadron, Sixth Cavalry Regiment".

George Weichmann took the envelope and led the boy to the captain's house nearby. The captain himself was not at home but his servants invited the shoemaker and his new charge to wait for his return. When the captain arrived a few hours later, he found his house in a state of great commotion. The boy's behaviour had grown more and more peculiar. He had spat out the beer and sausages offered to him — he seemed never to have seen such things before — but he wolfed down a meal of plain black bread and water. He seemed ravenously hungry. For some reason, he was terrifed of the captain's grandfather clock and burnt his hand when he tried to touch a candle flame. The shoemaker tried to talk to him, but he answered every question with "I don't know", "I don't know".

When the captain arrived home, the boy seemed fascinated by his uniform. It seemed to remind him of something important. Eventually, he managed to grunt a few words. "I want to be a soldier, like father . . .," he mumbled. "Horse . . . home . . . father." He also managed to write his name . . . Kaspar Hauser.

But who was this Kaspar Hauser and where had he come from? What had happened to him before his sudden and mysterious appearance in Nuremberg? Perhaps the envelope held the

answers. The shoemaker handed it over to the captain. It contained not one, but two letters. The first letter began:

"*Honoured Captain, I send you a boy who wishes to serve his king in the army. He was left with me on 7 October 1812. I am only a poor labourer with ten children of my own to raise. His mother asked me to bring the boy but I have enough to do with my own. Since he came, I have not let him out of the house. . .If you do not want to keep him, you can kill him or hang him up the chimney."* It ended by saying that if his parents had lived, he might have had the chance of a good education, for he was quick to learn and could do anything after being shown only once. The letter was unsigned but dated 1828.

The second letter was dated 1812, sixteen years earlier. It claimed to have been written by the boy's mother and was, presumably, the letter given to the poor labourer. It read:

"This child has been baptised. Please take care of him. His name is Kaspar. You must give him a second name yourself. His father was a cavalry soldier. When he is seventeen, take him to Nuremberg to the Sixth Cavalry regiment – his father belonged to it. He was born on 30 April 1812. I am a poor girl. I cannot take care of him."

The Captain decided that there was nothing he could do for the boy. The last thing he wanted in his regiment was the scandal attached to a long-lost, illegitimate child. So he handed Kaspar over to the city authorities.

They, in turn, handed him over to the police who locked him in a cell, under the watchful eye of a kindly and curious gaoler. He took the boy into his own home and tried to coax him to talk about his past life.

The gaoler noticed several strange things about the boy in his care. Kaspar seemed perfectly content to sit in his cell, on his own, without moving. When he did get up and walk, he was unsteady on his feet, like a young child learning to take its first steps. And his feet were so tender and soft that the shoes he was wearing had made them bleed. His skin was pale as if he had never seen the daylight. Indeed, he seemed far more at home at night and could even see in the dark. All this seemed to bear out what the "poor labourer" had written in his letter, that Kaspar had spent his whole life indoors with very little contact with other people or with the outside world.

But the gaoler firmly believed that, beneath his strange, child-like behaviour, lay a bright, intelligent boy who simply needed love and kindness to bring him out of himself. To prove his point, he bought Kaspar a toy wooden horse which the boy loved. He dressed it in ribbons and played with it for hours. Within six weeks, he had learned a string of new words and even began to speak in a few, broken sentences. He became more alert and aware of what was going on about him and began to respond more brightly and positively to what people said to him. Under his gaoler's watchful eye, he lost much of his earlier clumsiness and learned how to write with a quill pen and to use a pair of scissors – skills he had not been able to master before.

As Kaspar learned to speak, he slowly began to tell the gaoler more about himself and about his past life. His story was more astonishing than anything the gaoler had ever heard before. He listened with bated breath. Kaspar told him that, for as long as he could remember, he had lived in a tiny room, barely high enough to stand upright in. The windows were kept boarded up and he slept on a pile of straw on the floor. He always lay or sat down; he never walked about anywhere, which explained his stumbling steps. Each morning, he found that someone had left a jug of water and a piece of bread by his side. He said that the water often tasted bitter and made him fall asleep. When he awoke, he found that he had been dressed in a clean shirt and that his nails had been cut. He was given two wooden horses to play with but he was never allowed outside the tiny room and never saw the daylight. Indeed, before arriving in Nuremberg, he had only ever seen one other human being in his life.

This was a mysterious, masked stranger who came to his room one day and showed him how to write his name. He also taught him to say that he wanted to be a soldier like his father. Then he lifted him up and carried him outside where the bright light and fresh air made the boy faint. The next thing Kaspar remembered was finding himself wandering across the square in Nuremberg. He had no idea where he had come from or how he had got to Nuremberg, only that he must have been abandoned somewhere near the outskirts of the city.

Kaspar's extraordinary story made him famous throughout the city and beyond. Soon interest in his case had spread right across Europe. The boy from nowhere became a national celebrity. Doctors, lawyers and politicians came from far and wide to visit him, convinced that he was someone special, possibly even a long-lost member of the German royal family. All this interest was good for the town, and the Mayor and town council of Nuremberg decided to take Kaspar into their own care; he would be fed, clothed and housed at public expense. An appeal was sent out for information about the boy. Meanwhile, he was placed under the guardianship of a university professor, George Daumer, who had gained a reputation for his work in education and philosophy. Under his guidance, Kaspar grew into a healthy, intelligent, and seemingly normal young man. Kaspar enjoyed being the centre of attention, but perhaps that was only to be expected when so little attention had been paid to him in the past. Visitors flocked to see him, among them the famous lawyer, Anselm Ritter von Feuerbach. He reached a startling conclusion – that Kaspar was the illegitimate heir of the Duke of Baden. Kaspar bore an uncanny resemblance to the duke's family, von Feuerbach said. And his long and cruel imprisonment could easily be explained if he had been illegitimate – the duke would have wanted him out of the way to spare the family further embarrassment.

Before the claim could be further investigated, the story took another bizarre turn. On 7 October 1829, Kaspar was found, lying unconscious in Professor Daumer's cellar, bleeding from a stab wound to his head. When he came round, he told the professor that he had been attacked by a man wearing a black

silk mask. The news caused a sensation. Some people claimed that it was obviously an assassination attempt, put in motion by none other than the Duke of Baden, supposedly Kaspar's real father. But no attacker was ever found to fit the description, though the police mounted a thorough search. For many people in the town, however, the novelty of having the unknown boy in their midst was beginning to wear thin. They muttered that there had never been an assailant – the boy must have been making it up – and the wound must have been self-inflicted. Besides which, why should they carry on paying for the boy's upkeep? But the town council decided that Kaspar's life was indeed in serious danger. The boy was moved from Professor Daumer's house and taken to a new, secret address, where he stayed for two years, in hiding, still supported by public funds despite the grumblings of the townspeople.

Then, in May 1831, a wealthy and eccentric English aristocrat, Lord Stanhope, arrived in Nuremberg. He visited Kaspar many times and the two became firm friends, at least to start with. Lord Stanhope applied to the city authorities for permission to become Kaspar's guardian. His request was granted – the pressure of public opinion had been steadily mounting and the authorities were only too pleased to get Kaspar off their hands. Like von Feuerbach before him, Lord Stanhope was convinced that Kaspar was descended from royal blood. He treated him as if he were an aristocrat, wining and dining him in all the best restaurants and driving him around in his splendid carriage. In 1831, he took Kaspar on a grand tour of Europe. For two years, the pair visited one duke, earl or count after another. Kaspar was paraded in front of countless prying eyes and asked endless questions about his life. Relations between the two men soon became strained. Kaspar became increasingly vain and demanding, and Stanhope grew tired of him. When they returned to Nuremberg, Stanhope asked permission to lodge Kaspar in the nearby town of Ansbach where he would be tutored by Lord Stanhope's friend, a Dr Meyer. He employed a bodyguard, Captain Hickel, to watch over Kaspar. Then, feeling that he had fulfilled his part of the bargain, Lord Stanhope disappeared back to England.

Kaspar was miserable and lonely in Ansbach. Meyer was a mean-minded and suspicious man; Hickel was a bully and a thug. Kaspar longed for the glitter and glamour of his old life with Lord Stanhope – the dinner parties and carriage rides, the flattering attention and interest. By contrast, Dr Meyer scolded him constantly for not paying better attention to his lessons.

Then, just before Christmas 1833, Kaspar Hauser died, in circumstances equally as mysterious as his arrival in Nuremberg had been five years earlier. On 11 December, he was viciously attacked by a stranger as he was walking in a local park. He staggered into Dr

Meyer's house, gasping, "Man stabbed . . . knife . . . go quickly." He was bleeding profusely from a stab wound just below his ribs. A doctor was called at once and discovered that the knife had damaged Kaspar's lung and liver. In the park where Kaspar was stabbed, the police later found a black wallet which the attacker had dropped in his haste to get away. Inside the wallet was a note, written in mirror writing, which said:

"Hauser will be able to tell you how I look, where I came from and who I am. To spare him from this task, I will tell you myself. I am from . . . on the Bavarian border . . . My name is MLO."

But Kaspar could not remember anything about the man nor could he help to identify him. All he could tell them was that a workman had brought a message telling him to go to the park. When he got there, a tall, bearded man in a long, black cloak had asked him his name. When Kaspar told him, the man plunged a knife into the boy's ribs.

And that was all he could reveal. Some people began to doubt his story – only one set of footprints was found in the snow-covered park and they belonged to Kaspar. Could he have stabbed himself in a desperate cry for attention? A few days later, on 17 December,

Kaspar died. His last words were: "I didn't do it myself." He was buried in a quiet country churchyard where his gravestone read:

"Here lies Kaspar Hauser, enigma. His birth was unknown, his death mysterious".

It is reported that the Grand Duchess of Baden, rumoured to be Kaspar's real mother, wept when news reached her of the boy's death. Her husband had been the last of the direct line of dukes and, without an heir to succeed him, his title would now pass to the children of the rival Countess of Hochberg on his death. The story went that when the grand duchess gave birth to a son, the countess switched him for the dead baby of a palace servant. The healthy baby was given to a Major Hennenhofer who placed him in the care of a former soldier of his. On his deathbed, Hennenhofer is said to have confessed that that baby boy was none other than Kasper Hauser. Many things point to this being the true version of events. But we shall never know for sure, for all the major's private papers were destroyed when he died.

WHAT HAPPENED TO THE MEN OF EILEAN MORE?

"It's difficult to know where to begin, really. It was such a strange thing to happen, I still can't believe it to this day. It was just before Christmas, the 15th of December to be precise, at about nine o'clock in the morning. I'll never forget it. The light from the lighthouse on Eilean More suddenly went out, just like that. And the lighthouse keepers disappeared without trace.

Perhaps I'd better tell you a bit about Eilean More before I go any further. It's a bleak sort of place to the west of the Hebrides, in the Atlantic Ocean, the largest of the Flannan Islands. In fact, its name means "Big Island". Sailors called the Flannans the "Seven Hunters". They were named after St Flannan, a bishop, I think, if I remember the history we learnt at school. He built a small chapel on Eilean More – you won't see it now though, it's long gone. Local folk used to take their sheep over to the island, there's good grazing to be had there. But they always came back the same day. No one ever stayed there – they'd heard that the island was haunted by the little people and they weren't taking any chances. Anyway, the islands soon became famous as wrecking grounds. So many ships were wrecked on the rocks that in 1895 the Lighthouse Board (my employers) decided to build a lighthouse on Eilean More. It wasn't easy. The seas are rough in those parts and they had to haul all the materials they needed up a sheer cliff. The work took much longer than they'd anticipated – instead of two years, it took four – and the lighthouse only opened in 1894, in December. For a year, all went well and the lighthouse's beam certainly saved many ships from disaster. Then, last December, as I said, the light suddenly went out.

The Board ordered an immediate investigation into the matter but the seas were too stormy for us to launch the steamer from Lewis. I remember pacing up and down the seafront, not knowing what to think or do. I'd known the three lighthouse keepers – James Ducat, Donald McArthur and Thomas Marshall – since we were children and I was worried about them. They were good men. Something dreadful must have happened to prevent any of the three of them lighting the lamp. But what?

On Boxing Day, the sea was calmer and we

were able to sail from the harbour shortly after dawn. My mind was racing. I hadn't slept a wink the night before and I couldn't face anything to eat. I can't explain it but I had a really sick feeling in the pit of my stomach. With some difficulty, we managed to moor the ship by the eastern jetty. There was no sign of life, despite the signals we sent out. My sense of dread deepened. I ran up to the lighthouse gate and shouted. No reply. The main door was closed and no one answered my knock. When I opened the door and went inside, still calling to the keepers, I found the place empty and abandoned. The ashes in the fireplace were cold and the main clock had stopped. I waited for the others before venturing upstairs, only to find the sleeping quarters empty and the beds neatly made. On closer inspection, everything else in the lighthouse seemed normal. The last entry in the lighthouse records was 15 December – the day the light went out. But why had it gone out? Had the oil supplies used to light the lamp run out? No – we found oil a-plenty and the lights ready and waiting to be lit. Something must have happened, and happened suddenly, to prevent the keepers carrying out their duties.

Of course, I've heard the rumours which have done the rounds since then that the men must have been swept out to sea but 15 December was a calm, still day. It just doesn't make sense.

A few days later, another team of investigators landed on Eilean More and tried to piece together exactly what had happened. It was they who first suggested that the keepers had been swept away by a giant wave. The jetty showed evidence of storm damage and two sets of oilskins were missing – had the keepers put them on to inspect the damage before being washed away? But what happened to Donald McArthur? His oilskins were still in their place in the lighthouse? Had he rushed to save them and also been swept away? I can only repeat what I've said before, that on 15 December all was calm. The storms and rough seas didn't start until the next day. When the light went out, the seas around Eilean More were still.

Everyone seems to have their own opinion about what happened. Did one of them slip into the sea, and the others jump in to save him from drowing? I don't think so. These were experienced keepers – they were always very careful about their safety. Besides, there were plenty of ropes and lifeboats always hanging from the jetty. Another suggestion – one that makes me very angry – is that one of

them went mad, killed the others, then killed himself. As I said before, I've known these men since childhood. They were friends of mine and I can vouch for the fact that they were sound in body and mind. There's no evidence for any of these theories put about by folk that didn't know them, no clues, nothing. It's not something I'll ever forget, I can tell you. All I know is that I've lost three good friends – the experts can say what they like.

They must have gone somewhere, mustn't they?.After all, people don't just vanish into thin air, do they? Or *do* they?"

CHAPTER 5

RIDDLES OF THE PAST

DID THE CURSE OF THE PHARAOH COME TRUE?

On 26 November 1922, the British archaeologist, Howard Carter peered by candlelight through a small hole in the door of the tomb of King Tutankhamun in the Valley of the Kings in Egypt. "Can you see anything?" asked the man standing next to him, unable to bear the suspense for a moment longer. "Yes," Carter replied, with bated breath. "Wonderful things."

Behind the door of the tomb, closed to the prying eyes of the world for more than three thousand years, lay a breathtaking trove of gold and treasures, buried with the young boy-king who had ruled Egypt from 1333–1323 BC. The most wonderful find of all – the mummified body of King Tutankhamun himself, his face covered by a fabulous death mask of gold and precious stones – lay beyond the treasure in an inner burial chamber, yet to be discovered. The man who stood next to Howard Carter as he first set eyes on the boy-king's treasures did not live to see the mummy. For, six months after the tomb's discovery, Lord Carnarvon, passionate Egyptologist and patron of Howard Carter, was dead.

Officially, Carnarvon's death was blamed on an illness arising from an infected mosquito bite. In April 1923, Carnarvon had travelled to Aswan for some much-needed rest and relaxation. The excitement of the discovery of Tutankhamun's tomb had left him delighted but exhausted. One morning, as he was shaving, he nicked a mosquito bite on his cheek with his cut-throat razor. The bite quickly became infected. By breakfast next morning, Carnarvon was running a temperature of 104°F. For twelve days, the fever continued to rage. Then, just as he seemed about to recover, he suffered a serious relapse. He finally died from a bout of pneumonia as he lay on his sick-bed in a Cairo hotel. He was 57 years old.

Lord Carnarvon had only been present at the opening of Tutankhamun's burial chamber. The actual body of the boy-king was not revealed until two years after his death. But sinister rumours began to circulate almost immediately after he died, and people's imaginations were gripped by wild tales and even wilder speculation. The rumour-mongers blamed Lord Carnarvon's death not on natural causes at all but on the terrible Pharaoh's Curse, the dreadful revenge of a long-dead king of Egypt against those who had dared to disturb his tomb. Could it possibly be that

Carnvarvon was paying the ultimate price for ignoring the warning carved in ancient hiero-glyphs on a stone above his head as he entered the tomb? The warning read:

"Death will slay with his wings whoever disturbs the peace of the pharaoh."

Had this ancient warning finally come true?

What is certainly true is that a series of bizarre and unexplained events surrounded Lord Carnarvon's death. It is said that, at the exact moment he died in the Continental Hotel in Cairo, every light in the city went out at the same time and the nurse attending him was forced to light the room with candles. If further proof was needed that things were not quite what they seemed, it was not long com-ing. Thousands of kilometres away from Egypt, in Hampshire, England, at Lord Carnarvon's country house, his favourite dog, a fox terrier, began to howl and bark. At the exact moment of its master's death, at five to two in the morning, it gave one final, blood-curdling whine, rolled over on its side and died. Stranger still was the fact that the doc-

tors who examined Tutankhamun's mummy two years after Carnarvon's death reported finding a scab-like mark on the dead king's left cheek. Bizarrely, it was in exactly the same place as the mosquito bite which is said to have led to Lord Carnarvon's death.

Could all of this possibly be put down to an ancient curse unleashed on the world when Carter and Carnarvon entered the tomb months before and began the long and painstaking process of removing and cataloguing the priceless treasures of the pharaoh? Or was it simply a matter of coincidence, or even worse, a sensational story invented by the journalists purely to sell their papers? Two other pieces of information seemed to point towards the curse. Lord Carnarvon had been only too well aware of the power and influence of the Egyptian high-priests who presided over the rites of burial in ancient times. Fearful of his safety if he disturbed the tomb of a pharaoh, he had in fact consulted a famous mystic before setting off for Egypt to join Howard Carter. The mystic's words did not offer him the comfort he required. Instead, they held a warning:

"Lord Carnarvon, do not enter tomb. Disobey at peril. If ignored will suffer sickness. Not recover. Death will claim him in Egypt."

But the lure of the pharaoh's treasures and the glory of discovering one of the Valley of the King's last remaining tombs proved too tempting. Lord Carnarvon ignored the warning.

Many of the events surrounding the mysterious death of Lord Carnarvon could easily be passed off as a series of coincidences which made a good story for writers and journalists.

But, in the months following 1923, the curse was also blamed for the deaths of several other people who had all visited the tomb or been connected with it in some way. Shortly after Lord Carnarvon's death, his half-brother, Aubrey Herbert, died of peritonitis. Another archaeologist and a leading member of the expedition, called Arthur Mace, lapsed into a deep coma after complaining that he felt exhausted and weak. He died soon afterwards, leaving the doctors who treated him completely baffled about what had killed him. Mace had helped Carter with the work of unsealing the tomb. Like Carnarvon, Mace had been staying at the Hotel Continental in Cairo when he died.

More deaths followed in equally suspicious circumstances. An Egyptian prince, Ali Farmy Bey, was murdered in a London hotel and his brother committed suicide soon afterwards. The family claimed to be descended from the pharaohs themselves. George Jay Gould, an American railway tycoon, and a close friend of Lord Carnarvon, travelled to Egypt when he heard that Carnarvon had died, to see if there was any help he could offer. Before finally going on to Cairo, he stopped at the Valley of the Kings for a few days and asked Howard Carter to take him to look at the tomb. During his visit, he caught cold, and collapsed the following day with pneumonia. Twelve hours later, he was dead. Another casualty of the tomb was Carnvarvon's personal secretary, Richard Bethell, who had helped Howard Carter to catalogue the treasures found in the tomb. He was found dead in bed four months after the tomb was opened. He is thought to have died from heart failure, but there were also rumours that he may have committed suicide. He was just 49 years old. A few months later, his father, Lord Westbury, mysteriously fell to his death from the balcony of his London flat. On a table in his bedroom stood an alabaster vase taken from King Tutankhamun's tomb.

Six short years after the discovery of Tutankhamun's tomb, more than a dozen people who had been involved with its discovery in one way or another died from unnatural and unexplained causes. Seven years later, only two of the original team of excavators were still alive.

One man, however, continued to pour scorn on the idea of a legendary curse, and he had more cause than most to fear it. Howard Carter himself, the original discoverer of the tomb, died in March 1939, at a ripe old age, of entirely natural causes.

Yet, the curse was never far from the minds of those concerned with the tomb and its contents. It continued to claim its victims. In 1966, the Egyptian government finally agreed to send the treasures of Tutankhamun to Paris for an exhibition. Egypt's Director of Antiquities at the time, Mohammed Ibrahim, argued against letting the treasures go. He pleaded for the treasures to remain in Cairo because he had dreamt that his life would be in terrible danger if he allowed them to leave the country. After one last desperate meeting with the authorities in Cairo, during which he once again voiced his bitter opposition to the government's decision, he stepped out on to what looked like a clear road, was hit by a car and died instantly.

Four years later, the treasures were transported to London to be displayed at the British Museum. Millions of people flocked to see them. Even then, the curse continued to strike. Its first victim was Dr Gamal Mehrez, who had succeeded Mohammed Ibrahim as Director of Antiquities in Cairo. He scoffed at the notion of a curse and dismissed all the deaths and misfortune supposedly caused by it as examples of pure coincidence. But the night after supervising the packing of the treasures for their journey to England, he too was dead. Several other members of the plane which transported the treasures from Egypt were also dogged by misfortune. Three of them suffered heart attacks; one broke his leg; another had his home and belongings destroyed in a fire.

And so the mystery remains. Can the saga of deaths and misfortunes which has surrounded the discovery of the greatest ancient tomb ever be put down to coincidence? Could the explanation really be as innocent as that? Is the curse of the pharaoh really a case of myth and make-believe? Or have the guardians of the tomb succeeded in wreaking their terrible revenge on those whose dared disturb their dead ruler's final resting place?

WHY WAS THE GREAT PYRAMID BUILT?

By King Tutankhamun's time, the great pharaohs of Egypt had moved their burial places to escape the attentions of unscrupulous grave robbers. Instead of being laid to rest inside mighty stone pyramids, they were buried in underground tombs, cut into the rock of the Valley of the Kings, a barren, desolate place near the city of Thebes. But the pyramids remained – an astonishing testimony to the skills of the Ancient Egyptian builders and to the vision of their rulers. The most astonishing of all was the Great Pyramid of Cheops, built almost five thousand years ago, on the banks of the River Nile at Giza, just outside Cairo.

When an ancient scholar drew up a list of the seven most extraordinary buildings of their time, the Great Pyramid of Giza took pride of place among them. Today, it is the only one of the Seven Wonders of the World to survive. Built as a tomb for the great king, Cheops, who died in about 2528 BC, it is a monument worthy of the mightiest ruler. Constructed from over two million huge stone blocks, laid in place by workers using only the simplest tools, the pyramid covers an area of more than 5 hectares and stands 146 metres high, taller than the huge Church of St Peter's in Rome. An army of more than twenty thousand labourers toiled long and hard – some estimates put the building time at thirty years – to complete the pyramid in time for the king's burial. Cheops had begun elaborate preparations for his death while he was still very much alive. His dream was to be buried in the grandest pyramid ever seen, surrounded by his finest treasures, at the start of his soul's journey to the realm of the great Sun God, Ra.

While the Great Pyramid is undoubtedly an astonishing feat of engineering and construction, and a fitting tomb for a great king, some people think that there is much more to it than that. What was it *really* built for? Was it purely a burial place or was it something more than that? The largest of a group of pyramids at Giza, some people believe that the Great Pyramid is not only a tomb, but probably the world's oldest astronomical observatory, doubling up as an ancient calendar to register time passing not only in hours, but in days, seasons and even centuries, with astonishing accuracy.

In 1853, the French physicist, Jean Baptiste Biot visited Giza and began a long investigation of the pyramid. He came to the conclusion that the pyramid was, in fact, a gigantic sundial. But this was no ordinary sundial. It recorded far more than the time of day, for the builders of Ancient Egypt had built it with such incredible precision, on such a huge scale and in such a position, that it could also show the precise day of the year.

The north and south faces of the pyramid are bordered by wide, level pavements, called "shadow floors". In winter, the pyramid would have cast its shadow on the north-facing floor; in summer, the southern face would have reflected a triangle of sunlight on to the southern pavement. The paving blocks had been cut in such a way that the length of each day could be measured out. Ancient astronomers could also have used the sundial to forecast the year's equinoxes and solstices. These are two days each year when the sun crosses the Equator (the equinoxes), and two days each year when the sun is furthest away from the Equator (the solstices).

Another nineteenth century scientist, the British astronomer, Richard A. Proctor, seemed to support Biot's findings. He claimed that the Great Pyramid would have made a perfect astronomical observatory. As evidence, he pointed out that the great gallery, which leads deep in the heart of the pyramid and down into the burial chamber, is set at precisely the right angle to align it with the Pole Star, a crucial point of orientation for the study of the stars. Proctor also suggested that the gallery would have proved the ideal observation platform from which the astronomers of Ancient Egypt could watch the skies and record the movements of the stars and planets.

It is certainly possible that the pyramids were built with this two-fold function in mind. The Ancient Egyptians were highly skilled, highly advanced astronomers. They were able to identify the five planets known at that time, and to tell the difference between planets and stars, long before the invention of telescopes and other astronomical instruments. They used their knowledge to work out several calendars. The first was based on the stars. When Sirius (the Dog Star) rose in the sky just before sunrise, it signalled the start of the annual flood of the River Nile. The floodwaters were vital for watering the farmers' fields, so important, in fact, that the appearance of Sirius became the date of the Egyptian New Year. Their second calendar was based on the phases of the Moon, with each lunar month consisting of about 29.5 days. This was used to calculate the dates of some religious rites and festivals. The Egyptians were also the first people to divide the year into 365 days, which is still the basis of our calendar today, and which shows just how far advanced and how accurate were the findings of their astronomers.

Other people have suggested even more mysterious reasons for the construction of the Great Pyramid. One of the most bizarre of these was the theory put forward

by the Scottish Astronomer Royal, Charles Piazzi Smyth, in 1864. After a visit to the Great Pyramid, Smyth published his findings in a best-selling book entitled *Our Inheritance in the Great Pyramid*. He argued that the Great Pyramid had been built as a gigantic fortune-telling device. If its measurements, both inside and out, were decoded, they would predict the history of humankind from the very beginning of time right up to the Second Coming of Christ. He called his new theory "pyramidology".

Needless to say, there were plenty of people who dismissed Smyth's theories as nonsense. But whichever theory you choose to believe, even if you believe in none at all, one thing cannot be denied. Nothing like the pyramids has ever been built since then, nor is ever likely to be built in the future. And their magic is as powerful now as it was in the days of the Ancient Egyptians who built them – wonders of the world, indeed.

STONEHENGE —
What is the secret of the Stones?

The great circle of gigantic stones which stands tall and proud on Salisbury Plain, in Wiltshire, England, has been a source of mystery and speculation since ancient times. How did the stones get there? Why were they erected here? And what purpose was the stone circle built for? What secrets do the stones contain?

It is thought that the building of Stonehenge took place in three distinct stages, beginning in about 2700 BC, with a group of Neolithic, or New Stone Age, builders. They built the ditch and the bank which encircle the stone complex. They also set up the great "heel stone" which is aligned so precisely that, on midsummer's day, the first rays of the sun strike it and the central point of the two stone circles (Stonehenge was originally formed of two stone circles, one inside the other). Some nine hundred years later, the Beaker People, so-called because of their custom of burying pottery artefacts with their dead, moved into the site. They are said to have hauled and erected the mighty bluestones, sixty huge slabs weighing four tonnes each. These were arranged in a double circle inside the earlier enclosure. The stones were probably brought from South Wales, some 480 kilometres away, on an elaborate series of rollers and sledges, the most advanced technology available in the days before the invention of the wheel. The inner "trilithons" (two upright stones with a cross bar placed across the top) were hoisted into place in about 1500 BC, by Bronze Age people from Wessex. The construction of this extraordinary monument is thought to have been completed by about 1400 BC.

Many different theories have been put forward about the true purpose of Stonehenge, one of several similar stone circles which are found right across Europe. Until quite recently, it was generally believed that Stonehenge had been built by the Druids, members of an ancient religious cult, as a temple for worshipping the sun and as a place for performing human sacrifices. But archaeologists have now discovered that Stonehenge was built more than a thousand years before the Druids. It may well have been used by them – it is still sacred to their modern descendants – but it could not have been built by them. So why was it originally built?

In 1963, the American astronomer, Professor Gerald Hawkins, put forward his latest, startling theory. It proved to be extremely controversial and continues to be so today. Hawkins claimed that he had finally solved the mystery of the great stones and suggested that, in his opinion, Stonehenge had been built as some type of giant, prehistoric computer-cum-observatory. Its function was to carry out complicated calculations about the movements and positions of the sun, moon and stars. When Hawkins fed all the data he had collected about Stonehenge into his own computer, he discovered that the stones could also be used to predict when eclipses of the sun and moon would occur (these were seen as very bad omens by ancient people). He suggested that, by moving smaller, marker, stones around the stones of the outer circle, ancient astrologers and priests would be able to plot the movements of the heavenly bodies and to use their findings to work out the best times for planting and harvesting crops, forecasting the weather and, crucially, for predicting the future.

At first, his theory was dismissed as being too far-fetched to be taken seriously. But, gradually, it began to gain ground. After all, thirty years before Hawkins first proposed his theory, another academic, Alexander Thom, had already suggested that the stones of Stonehenge were so precisely placed and aligned, that they must have been used as

some form of astronomical observatory. If the Great Pyramid, built seven hundred years before work on Stonehenge even began, could have been an observatory, why not this massive stone circle?

In 1976, the observatory theory found another supporter, in a Scottish archaeologist, Dr Euan Mackie. He announced that he had found the site, near Stonehenge, of an academy where ancient astronomer-priests had been trained. It would have been highly educated men like these who had stood in the centre of the stone circle and interpreted the positions of the sun and moon, using the stones as a guide.

Other famous astronomers agreed that the

stones could have been used as markers to track the position of the moon as it moved through the phases of its monthly cycle. Far from being built by primitive farmers and labourers, as had previously been assumed, it seemed that Stonehenge was the work of a brilliant group of priests and intellectuals who were able to carry out complicated calculations long before they had the means of writing them down

WHO WAS BURIED AT NEWGRANGE?

Early on a winter's day in 1969, after seven years of patient and painstaking excavation, the Irish archaeologist, Michael Kelly, stood in the dark, cave-like chamber inside the prehistoric grave mound of Newgrange in Ireland . . . and waited. It was 21 December, the shortest day of the year and the day of the winter solstice. At two minutes before 9 a.m., his years of hard work were rewarded. As the sun rose in the sky outside, a pencil-thin beam of sunlight shone through a narrow slit in the roof, and along the passage, gradually getting wider and wider, and filling the gloomy chamber in which Kelly was standing with light.

The extraordinary scene Kelly witnessed must have been familiar to the builders of Newgrange five thousand years ago. For, like Stonehenge, Newgrange appears to have been built as an ancient calendar, deliberately constructed to be aligned with a key moment in the solar year. In this case, that moment was the start of the winter solstice, a day which marked the end of the darkest part of the year, bringing longer, lighter days and the promise of spring.

But Newgrange had also been built as a prehistoric grave, a passage grave, one of the finest found in Europe. The saucer-shaped burial mound itself was built from thousands of stones from the nearby river, about the size of large oranges, closely packed with layers of turf. It was enclosed by a circle of massive standing stones. Inside the mound, the burial chamber in which Michael Kelly stood lies at the end of a narrow, 20-metre-long passage, which is lined with slabs of stone. Here, archaeologists found the remains of some ancient human bones and various beads, bone tools and jewellery, which they believed to be funeral offerings. Off the main chambers are three small recesses. Guarding the entrance is a huge, elaborately carved and patterned curb-stone. The mound stands on a ridge overlooking the River Boyne. Around it, the countryside is dotted with about twenty small and two large grave mounds, all dating from the Stone Age in about 3200 BC.

The life of the mound's prehistoric builders, and the identity of the grave's occupants, however, remains shrouded in mystery. An ancient Irish legend links Newgrange with the Irish god, Dagda, who was called the "Good God". He belonged to a mythical race of people who are said to have lived all over Ireland until the arrival of the Celts some time after AD 500, when they mysteriously disappeared. Newgrange then passed to Dagda's son who had the body of a legendary hero called Dairmaid brought there for burial by a team of fairy horsemen.

Another legend says that, in historical times, Newgrange was the burial place of the Irish high kings of Tara (which lies some 20 kilometres to the south west), who lived in the days before the Christians arrived in Ireland in the fifth century AD. One of these kings, Cormac mac Airt, is said to have given strict orders that his body was not to be buried in

Newgrange. He thought that it was an ungodly place. But the king's servants ignored his request and, when he died, they carried his body in a grand procession to Newgrange. As they reached the River Boyne, which they had to cross to get to the burial mound, the king's body magically swelled up to three times its normal size, making it impossible for them to carry it across the river. So, they buried King Cormac on the river bank, and not in the mound, according to the his wishes.

Excavations carried out on the tomb have only added to the air of mystery surrounding Newgrange. The mound was rediscovered in 1699 by a local landowner who began to remove the stones one by one to build a road and discovered in the process the entrance to the passage. Since then, many archaeologists and historians have explored Newgrange and formed their own theories about the grave's past. In 1725, Thomas Molyneux, a professor from Trinity College, Dublin, claimed that the mound had been built in the Middle Ages, by Danish invaders. Other theories suggested that the ancient builders had been Egyptian or Indian. More recent evidence points to the mound having been constructed by invaders from Spain or France, where similar structures and building techniques have been found.

But was Newgrange simply a royal burial mound, or did it serve another purpose as an astronomical observatory. Perhaps it was designed so that the winter sun lit up the final resting place of the high kings, speeding their souls towards the next world. We shall probably never know . . .

HOW DID THE EASTER ISLAND STATUES GET THERE?

Easter Island is one of the loneliest spots on Earth. This tiny island lies in the Pacific Ocean, some 3,000 kilometres off the west coast of Chile, and over 1,500 kilometres from its nearest neighbour, Pitcairn Island. Standing on the island, with their backs to the deep-blue ocean, are an extraordinary display of gigantic stone heads, some six thousand in total, gazing out across the valleys and hills. Some stand tall; others have long since toppled over. Others have been abandoned further down the hillside, still in the process of being carved out of the solid rock. Many of the heads are massive, weighing over 50 tonnes. But how did the heads get there? Who were they carved by? And when were they carved? These are the questions which have baffled scientists and anthropologists alike for almost 250 years.

The first foreigner to see and record the amazing statues of Easter Islands was the Dutch admiral, Jacob Roggeveen who sailed past the island in 1722. On all his many voyages, Roggeveen had never seen anything like it in his life – an undiscovered island in the mid-South Pacific dotted with giants. As he sailed closer, he was relieved to see that the giants were carved from stone and the men he could see walking among them were of normal size. Next day, Roggeveen took a small landing party ashore for a closer inspection of the statues. They stood on a row of huge walls, like gigantic battlements, and each represented the bust of a man with very long ears and a red headpiece. As it was Easter Sunday, Roggeveen named the island, Easter Island. Then he sailed away again. It was almost fifty years before the next party of Europeans reached Easter Island, and another century before the island was considered worthy of serious exploration.

Since then, however, many people have tried to decipher the meaning behind these mysterious statues, with, so far, little success. What seems to be certain is that there were once many, many more heads than the thousands on view today. Some have been stolen; others have toppled into the sea; others have been destroyed during one of the many inter-tribal wars which broke out on the island in years gone by. Those that remain present an awe-inspiring spectacle, however. They are carved from dark volcanic rock from the crater of the island's sleeping volcano. More than three hundred of the heads had been carved from the walls of the crater, then lowered down the slope of the volcano. (Another four hundred unfinished heads were found still inside the crater.) They had then been manoeuvred somehow into a standing position on to the stone platforms. They range in size from just one metre in height to a towering 12 metres. Some heads, which have never been hauled upright, measure more than 20 metres. These still lie on the ground, surrounded by the chisels, hatchets and other tools which were used to carve their brooding features. Why they were abandoned so suddenly, and what happened to the workers who were mid-way through carving them, is a mystery yet to be solved. Had they intended to return one day to finish off their handiwork? We may never know.

Some of the statues lay several kilometres from the crater and experts are still unsure about how they were carried so far and hauled upright. Two theories were put forward. Had they been dragged into place on huge log rollers? This theory was quickly discounted when it was discovered that the poor soil of

Easter Island would not have been able to support trees of such an enormous size. Had the workers used vines woven into ropes to pull the statues across the ground? This too was ruled out when scientists proved that such ropes would not be strong enough to support such colossal weights.

A likely explanation of the mystery of why the statues have long ears does at least seem to have been found. Drawings have been found which seem to indicate that the ancient inhabitants of Easter Island were divided into two groups, or classes of society. The "long-eared" people, who used weighted earrings to stretch their ear lobes, were the rulers, and the "short-eared" people, their subjects.

The question of how the Easter Islanders happened upon such an isolated and remote location in the first place is almost as big a mystery as the heads themselves. The Norwegian explorer and anthropologist, Thor Heyerdahl, suggests that the people who carved the heads were invaders from the east who reached the island by raft, many years before the arrival, in about 1680, of the island's present Polynesian inhabitants. Once they reached the island, he suggests, they were not able to repair or rebuild their wooden rafts because there were so few trees on the islands. Unable to return to their homes, they settled on the island, putting their skills to good use in the carving of the heads. Over the years, however, their skills and culture began to die out. By the time, Jacob Roggeven reached the island in 1722, no one could remember who carved the heads or why.

Another theory suggests that Easter Island once formed part of a vast lost continent called Lemuria which is supposed to have stretched right across the Pacific Ocean. The heads might have been portraits of the people of Lemuria, who were believed to be giants. Yet another proposal is that they were put on the island by aliens from another planet!

Thousands of years after the heads were carved, however, we are no nearer to discovering their true meaning nor the identity of their ancient carvers. Their secret has long since disappeared, along with the extraordinary skills of their creators.

HOW DID THE DINOSAURS DIE OUT?

For 140 million years, dinosaurs ruled the world. They dominated every part of the Earth, its swamps, jungles, rivers and plains. Then, about 65 million years ago, these mighty reptiles suddenly and completely died out. And despite the efforts of hundreds of scientists all over the world, despite the hundreds of research papers written on the subject and the scores of meetings and conferences, no one is exactly sure why.

Here are some of the theories, sensible and otherwise, which attempt to explain the disappearance of the dinosaurs:

The (slightly more) sensible theories:
• Did the dinosaurs die of starvation? Perhaps the carnivorous (meat-eating) dinosaurs became such good hunters that they killed off all the plant-eating dinosaurs they lived on. Or did the plant-eaters die off for some reason, perhaps from eating poisonous plants, leaving the meat-eaters with nothing to eat?
• Did the dinosaurs simply grow too big for their own good? Fossil finds have

shown that some dinosaurs produced very large amounts of growth hormone. If this production became too great, it may have caused problems with their metabolisms.

• Were the dinosaurs killed off by a huge dose of radiation caused by the explosion of a star. If so, why were they the only group of animals affected?

• Were they wiped out by disease?

• Were they unable to survive because their brains were so small for their size? The huge Stegosaurus had a tiny brain, only about the size of a walnut. But scientists have found no evidence that dinosaurs were stupid despite the smallness of their brains. After all, they did survive perfectly well for some 75 million years, far longer than people have been around.

• Did early, egg-eating mammals eat the dinosaurs' eggs? They probably did eat some of their eggs but it seems unlikely that they could have eaten enough of them to cause the complete extinction of the dinosaurs.

The (downright) silly theories:

• Were the dinosaurs hunted and killed

by prehistoric cavemen? (In fact, they died out millions of years before human beings first appeared on Earth.)

• Were they left out of the reckoning when Noah gathered the animals into his Ark and drowned in the great flood?

• Were they kidnapped by alien beings in flying saucers. (Imagine the size of the flying saucers!)

• Did they commit mass suicide, like lemmings?

• And finally, silliest of all, did they simply grow tired of life and die of boredom?

Over the past ten years or so, another explanation has emerged which many, though not all, experts seem to agree with. This theory suggests that the end of the dinosaurs came when a gigantic meteorite crashed into the Earth, smashing open a massive crater and throwing enough dust into the atmosphere to lower temperatures around the world and affect the growth of the plants on which the dinosaurs and their prey lived. Alternatively, an enormous volcanic eruption may have been the reason for the vast dust clouds. Such a collision is certainly possible. The only problem is that no evidence of such an enormous meteorite crater has yet been found.

Other scientists suggest that the extinction of the dinosaurs was a long, slow process which took place over at least five million years, not all of a sudden as is often believed. This time-scale corresponds with the end of a warm period in the Earth's history, and the beginning of a cooler one. If, as is widely believed, the dinosaurs were cold-blooded reptiles, they may not have been able to survive the sudden drop in temperature. Even if they were warm-blooded, they may have met the same fate, as they did not have warm coats of fur or feathers to protect their bodies from the cold.

What do you think?

WHO WAS THE MAN IN THE ICE?

THE TIME: five thousand years ago.
THE PLACE: a mountain pass high up in the Alps.

A lonely traveller stops to rest in a rocky hollow, sheltered for a moment from the howling winds which sweep savagely down the mountain slopes. Ahead of him lie two valleys – one an awesome mass of icy glaciers leading to a raging river; the other, tree lined and edged with green meadows. Was this the valley that would take him home? Who was the man, and what had taken him so high into the mountains on this treacherous winter's day? Was he a shepherd, leading his sheep to their winter pastures in the valley below? Was he a travelling trader, on his way back home from selling his wares in a neighbouring village? Was he a priest, returning from a pilgrimage, or an outlaw, banished from his village home for some unknown crime? Perhaps he was a hunter, out collecting material for making weapons?

Whoever he was, and whatever his business, he was exhausted from his journey, cold and hungry. He was looking forward to a few minutes' rest. He sat down and unpacked his belongings from a bark rucksack he was carrying. Ravenously, he ate the only food he had with him — a piece of dried ibex meat, tough but nourishing, and a few berries. It would have to last until he reached home. He also had a few small pieces of charcoal for lighting a fire, but the wind was blowing too strongly and there was no wood to burn for miles around.

Then, for some reason, he placed his belongings one by one around the hollow. Perhaps he was caught by a sudden blizzard which transformed the windswept countryside and made it impossible for the man to get his bearings. Perhaps he was simply overcome by cold or exhaustion, his strength sapped by his long, hard journey and lack of food. Something prevented him going any further for a while, at least. The stranger stretched out across a wide, flat stone, lying on his left side, laid his head down and went to sleep.

He never woke up . . .

THE TIME: 19 September, 1991
THE PLACE: a mountain pass high up in the Alps.

Two German tourists, Helmut and Erika Simon, are coming down the mountain after a long hike through the Alps near the Austrian-Italian border. They have wandered slightly

off the usual trail, but they are experienced climbers and know that they can quickly rejoin the path if necessary. Suddenly, Erika Simon catches sight of a small head and pair of shoulders jutting out of the ice. The couple go over to investigate. They think that they have stumbled across the body of a missing climber, caught in a recent avalanche. After all, such things are not uncommon in these often treacherous mountains. In fact, unbeknown to them, they have found the icy grave of the prehistoric traveller, who has lain, entombed in the ice for more than five thousand years.

The discovery of the man in the ice certainly caused great interest and excitement but it was some time before his true age and identity were calculated. In fact, early attempts to free the body almost destroyed this remarkable find altogether. Like the Simons before them, the first people on the scene thought that they were digging out a twentieth-century avalanche victim, and not an ancient traveller. They dug enthusiastically but roughly and carelessly. As they tried to haul the body out with ice-axes and ski poles, they managed to destroy what was left of the man's clothing, snap his two-metre-long bow and leave a gaping hole in his hip. One digger had seized a nearby stick to dig with. The stick later turned out to be part of the traveller's backpack, the likes of which had never been seen before. Worse was to follow. As the man was pulled free of the ice, his genitals were snapped off. Then the body was slung into a sack and taken by air to the nearest Austrian village. Here it was crammed into a coffin, which was far too small for it, breaking its left arm in the process, for the car journey to Innsbruck. And, as the photographers in Innsbruck snapped away at the shrivelled body, a fungus began to grow on the man's skin.

Five days after the discovery of the body, it

was finally examined by the eminent archaeologist, Konrad Spindler, of the University of Innsbruck.

"I needed only one second," he later confessed, "to see that the body was four thousand years old."

Spindler based his estimate on the date of the man's axe – a wooden-handled weapon with a copper blade. In fact, the man was even older than he suspected. Radiocarbon tests showed him to have lived in about 3000 BC, making his one of the oldest and best-preserved bodies ever discovered, and his axe the oldest found in Europe which was still complete with its bindings and handle.

Urgent measures were now needed to prevent further damage to the body, preserved for so long by the ice that surrounded it. For safety, it was now placed in a freezer at the University, at the same temperature and in the same atmospheric conditions as the ice it was found in. The body was only allowed out for twenty minutes at a time, for brief examinations by scientists. For, by now, its true worth had at last been realized – this was one of the most important archaeological finds ever, a priceless clue to the past.

It was not long before the Iceman's fame spread and he became an international celebrity. He was nicknamed Ötzi, after the Ötzal valley which lay to the north of his icy grave. Within just a few months, the shops were filled with Ötzi T-shirts, postcards and other Iceman souvenirs. A pop song was even written about the Iceman. It seemed that everyone had their own weird or wonderful theory about Ötzi's identity. One suggestion was that he was an Egyptian mummy, stolen from the British Museum and buried in the ice as a hoax!

Gradually, as scientists continued their examination of the Iceman's body, more details emerged. For five thousand years, his body had lain in the rocky hollow where he had fallen asleep, some way away from the nearby glacier. This explained the astonishing condition in which the body was found – incredibly, the man's brain, eyeballs and internal organs were preserved intact, and scientists were even able to tell what he had eaten for his final meal. For bodies caught in glaciers are usually smashed and broken as the ice slides slowly but surely down the mountainside. Ötzi's icy tomb had saved him from this fate.

Apart from the axe, most definitely his most valuable possession, Ötzi had been carrying a wooden-handled flint dagger in a grass sheath, probably used for cutting up meat. He also had several flints and some pieces of charcoal for lighting fires, which were stored in a small pouch. His weapons consisted of a two-metre long bow and fourteen arrows in a deerskin quiver. A short stick tipped with deer antler was probably used for sharpening the flints. The Iceman's belongings had been stored in a backpack made of hazel-wood, larch-wood and bark. Only two of the arrows were complete and ready for firing, however, the Iceman's bow was unstrung and could not have been used. Had this been at the root of his problems? Had the Iceman damaged his weapons somehow and been searching the windswept mountainside for materials to make new bows and arrows?

And what did the Iceman look like? As scientists studied the body further, a fascinating picture began to emerge. Using computer images and X-rays, they were able to piece together a reconstruction of the Iceman's face, to show what he might have looked like when he had been alive. This is what they discovered. The man was in his twenties or thirties, stood 1.5 metres tall, and had dark, wavy brown hair and a short beard. When the hundred or so scraps of cloth had been painstakingly pieced together, scientists discovered that his tunic and trousers were made of animal skins; the cape he wore around his shoulders was made of plaited grass and his shoes were leather, stuffed with clumps of grass for warmth. Round his neck, he wore a leather thong, threaded with a stone bead which may have acted as an amulet or lucky charm. He was also carrying a piece of fungus tied to the end of a string. Scientists think that this might have been an ancient first-aid kit. Under his clothes, Ötzi had several, mysterious marks on his skin, like tattoos. There were several sets of blue, parallel lines on his back, a cross behind his left knee, and a series of stripes on one of his ankles. What the marks signified, however, the scientists could not tell. They had never seen anything like them before. Perhaps they were meant as identity marks, to show that Ötzi belonged to a particular tribe? Perhaps they had some religious or mystical meaning?

We will never know what led Ötzi to the freezing mountain peak nor what exactly led to his death. His body showed no signs of severe injury or disease, and it seems most likely that he froze to death as he slept in the rocky hollow. But the Iceman is undoubtedly one of the most important archaeological finds ever made. Further investigations showed that he lived between the Stone Age and the Copper Age, when prehistoric human beings were beginning, for the first time in their history, to make tools and weapons out of metal instead of stone. Copper, the material of Ötzi's axe, was the first metal to be widely used in prehistoric times when people discovered how it extract it by melting down copper ore. It proved much easier to work with than stone and people never looked back. The Stone Age was soon left behind and the course of human history changed forever.

DID THE FLOOD OF THE BIBLE ACTUALLY HAPPEN?

Over the centuries, many people, ranging from professional archaeologists to religious fanatics, have sought the answer to one of the world's most intriguing mysteries – did the great flood mentioned in the Bible actually happen? And was a man called Noah actually instructed by God to build a mighty Ark and fill it with animals to replace those that would perish in the flood?

"The winds blew for six days and nights, flood and tempest overwhelmed the world."

These words do not come from the Bible, although they are very similar to the account of the great flood found in the Book of Genesis. For accounts of a great flood appear in many cultures. All of them tell the story of a mighty deluge, sent by God, which threatened to destroy life on Earth as punishment for the wickedness of mankind. In each story, total and utter devastation is prevented only by the construction of a gigantic wooden boat – the Noah's Ark of the Bible.

The first account of a flood engulfing the Earth comes from the world's oldest written legend, *The Epic of Gilgamesh*, composed in Sumeria some five thousand years ago. In this story, a good and holy man called Uta Napishtim is chosen by the gods to survive the flood which they send to destroy the world. The god, Ea, warns Uta Napishtim what is going to happen. He tells him to build a great boat and load it with gold, silver, his family and cattle, and a selection of birds and beasts of the land. Uta Napishtim does as he is told. Then the rains begin to fall, as the gods have foretold, and continue to fall for six days and six nights. On the seventh day, the rains stop and the sea grows calm, "and all mankind was changed into mud." Uta Napishtim's boat comes to rest on the summit of Mount Nisir, the only land which has emerged from the waves. So, Uta Napishtim and his family survive, to fill the world with better, more god-fearing people like themselves.

In 1929, the famous British archaeologist, Sir Leonard Woolley, was excavating the ancient Sumerian city of Ur when he discovered a layer of clay, some 3.6 metres thick. He dated the clay and announced that it must have been deposited in about 3,500 BC, about five hundred years before *The Epic of Gilgamesh* was written. "So vast a mass of silt laid down at one time," Woolly suggested, "could only be the result of a very great flood." Unfortunately, other people shouted his theory down, pointing out that none of the nearby sites showed any evidence of flooding and that many parts of Ur had in fact survived, so the flood, if it had happened at all, had not been nearly as serious as Woolley supposed.

The story does not end there, however. Earlier this century, a prayer dating from about 2,200 BC was found during the excavation of another site. It recorded a devastating event:

"Waters pouring out – destroying cities like the flood wave."

Was this another piece of evidence that the flood did take place?

The story of Noah's Ark shows many similarities with the Sumerian account. Instead of Uta Napishtim, God chooses Noah, a good and holy man, to build a great boat and sail to safety. In the Bible, the flood lasts longer — forty days and forty nights — but, as in *The Epic of Gilgamesh*, the Ark eventually comes to rest on the top of a high mountain, this time Mount Ararat in Turkey. For centuries, people have searched Mount Ararat from top to bottom for any trace of the mysterious Ark.

The mountain rises 5,165 metres above a flat plain, some 950 kilometres to the east of the city of Ankara. Its summit is snow-covered and windswept. This has not stopped the Ark-hunters — since the fifth century, priests scaled the mountain and brought back, so they claimed, splinters of the tar-coated timbers from which the Ark is said to have been built.

In 1876, an Englishman, James Bryce, claimed to have found a larger piece of wood from the Ark on Mount Ararat. He took this as certain proof that the Ark had existed. If it hadn't come from the Ark, where had it come from? No trees had grown on the slopes of Mount Ararat for hundreds of years. In 1969, a French investigator, Fernand Navarre, made another astonishing discovery. He used the technique of radiocarbon dating to date some fragments of wood found on a previous expedition. He concluded that the wood was about five thousand years old. It was also found that the type of wood found did not come from any trees growing in the region around the mountain. It originated from Mesopotamia, where Noah is said to have lived!

In August 1984, an American explorer, Marvin Steffins, made an astonishing announcement. He had found Noah's Ark, he claimed, some 1,500 metres up Mount Ararat. From the air, Steffins said, you could clearly see the remains of the hull of an enormous ship which corresponded exactly to the dimensions of the Ark as they were set out in the Bible. He later visited the site and collected fragments of wood to back up his theory. But a full-scale excavation of the "Ark" has still to be undertaken.

As for the flood itself, there is some scientific research to show that it might indeed have happened. Until quite recently, scientists and archaeologists like Sir Leonard Woolley believed that it had been a local flood, affecting a small area around the ancient Sumerian city of Ur. They put forward the theory that an earthquake or cyclone caused the rivers Tigris and Euphrates to burst their banks and flood the surrounding land for many kilometres around. This event formed the basis of the flood story in *The Epic of Gilgamesh* and of Noah's Ark.

But experts now believe that the flood was not simply a local phenomenon, but a worldwide one. After studying ancient sediments dredged from the bed of the Gulf of Mexico, the geologist Cesare Emiliani concluded that "about 11,600 years ago, the North American ice cap underwent a sudden collapse followed by rapid melting. A huge amount of ice-melt water rushed into the Gulf of Mexico and produced a sea-level rise that spread around the world with the speed of a giant tidal wave, which can circle the globe in 24 hours. Man was forced to move inland, and this universal migration may have created the memory of a universal flood. We know this because the oxygen isotope ratios [of the sediment] show a marked temporary decrease in the salinity of the waters of the Gulf of Mexico. It clearly shows that there was a major period of flooding from 12,000 to 10,000 years ago, with a peak of about 11,600 years ago. There is no question that there was a flood and there is no question that it was a universal flood."

So, research does show that the legend

might actually be based on truth and that, at one time in the Earth's history, the world was swamped by a mighty flood, the like of which has never been seen again. For centuries it remained a powerful force in people's memories. This would explain the many flood stories which appear in the myths of ancient civilizations, which were used to teach people about the terrible consequences of wickedness. As to the existence of the Ark itself, opinions are divided. People who claim to have found fragments of the mighty boat are convinced that they have found the Ark in its final resting place on Mount Ararat. Some historians, however, believe that Noah would not have been able to collect enough wood locally to build such an enormous boat. They think that the Ark was constructed as a raft made of papyrus reeds, with a wooden shelter built on top. If that was the case, the reed raft would have perished long ago.

Did you know?

In the Hindu version of the flood story, a giant fish warns the hero Manu of the coming deluge and later pulls Manu's boat to safety.

Did you know?

There is an extraordinary entry in the register of the Atlantic Mutual Insurance Company in New York, USA. The company has one of the biggest archives of marine disasters in the world. The entry reads:

"Noah's Ark. Built in 2448 BC. Gopher wood, pitched within and without. Length: 300 cubits*; width: 50 cubits; height: 30 cubits. Three decks. Cattle carrier. Owner: Noah and sons. Last reported stranded on Mount Ararat."

*A cubit is an ancient measurement which originated in Ancient Egypt. Originally the length from a person's elbow to their middle fingertip (about 45 centimetres), it was later fixed at 53 centimetres.

THE WORLD'S MOST MYSTERIOUS MANUSCRIPT

In 1912, an extraordinary manuscript was discovered in an old chest in the Jesuit college of Mondragone in Frascati, Italy where it had lain for years, hidden and forgotten. What a treasure it turned out to be. It was slightly bigger than a modern paperback with 204 pages (another 28 pages had been lost). And it was written in code. The pages were also decorated with diagrams of the heavens showing the positions of the stars and planets, little drawings of female figures and jottings of strange-looking plants in a variety of different colours. The book was sold for a large sum to an American rare book dealer, Wilfred Voynich. It came to be known as the Voynich manuscript.

The manuscript was accompanied by an ancient letter, dated 19 August 1666 which was written by the rector of Prague University, Joannes Marcus Marci. The letter was addressed to the renowned Jesuit scholar, Athanasius Kircher, an expert in cryptography (the study of codes and ciphers). He had already been sent a few pages of the manuscript by its previous owner who had devoted his own life to attempting to decipher it. (Its present owner was no less a person than the Holy Roman Emperor Rudolf II of Prague.) Now Kircher was sent the whole manuscript. Little is known about the manuscript's history up to this point. One theory is that it was brought to Prague from England by the magician, John Dee. And according to Joannes Marcus Marci, the writer of the letter, the author of the manuscript was none other than Roger Bacon, the thirteenth-century scientist and monk.

Try as he might, Kircher was unable to decipher the manuscript despite several years of trying. With great disappointment, he returned it to the Jesuits. It had proved absolutely baffling – all the more so because at first sight it seemed so perfectly straightforward. The writing looked like ordinary medieval handwriting found in hundreds of similar books. But it wasn't. The pictures of the plants and planets suggested that it must be a medieval "herbal", a book which catalogued the healing properties of drugs. These were often illustrated with astronomical drawings because certain plants were best gathered at the time of the full moon, at sunrise, or when the stars and planets were in a certain position in the sky. But it wasn't a herbal, either.

Wilfred Voynich was convinced that modern scholars would stand a much better chance of deciphering the manuscript so he sent copies to the leading experts in the field. They began by trying to determine which language the manuscript was written in. The plants should have provided a clue to this but most of them proved to be imaginary, no help at all. Some of the star constellations shown in the astronomical diagrams were recognizable but the code could simply not be translated to reveal their known names. Certain letters and symbols were picked out as occurring the most number of times. But any attempt to link them to the most commonly used letters in any known alphabet proved unsuccessful. Astronomers, linguists, experts on Bacon, scholars from the Vatican itself – none were able to discover the secrets of the Voynich manuscript.

Then in 1921 came an exciting breakthrough, when William Romaine Newbold, professor of philosophy at the University of Pennsylvania, USA, announced that he had succeeded where the others had failed. He had finally cracked the code! According to him, the text was indeed a scientific work by Roger Bacon, written in straightforward Latin. The letters of each word had then been scrambled

up to produce a manuscript made up of ana-
grams. All it had needed was unscrambling.
Everyone accepted that Bacon had been an
extremely intelligent man. But Newbold's text
suggested that Bacon had been much more
than this, and had, in fact, made a series of
startling scientific discoveries long before his
time and long before the accepted dates for
these finds. Could he really have been the
greatest scientist ever, greater than Isaac
Newton or Galileo? And why had no one
known about this before?

Two years after Newbold's death, aged sixty
two years old in 1926, the results of his investigations were published by a friend. And they
were widely accepted as the true interpretation of the Voynich manuscript. But some
scholars were far from convinced. They pointed to flaws in the system Newbold had used to
decipher the text. It worked one way (i.e. to
translate the code into Latin) but it could not
possibly have worked the other way round (i.e.
when Bacon had turned the original text into
code). It just didn't make sense. Dr John
Manly, a linguist and recognized code-breaker
was called in. He had already proved his
worth by breaking codes used by German
spies during the First World War. Now he
turned his attention to the manuscript. His

conclusion? That, despite his obviously hon-
ourable intentions, Newbold had got it wrong.
His anagram theory was unworkable and his
interpretation of certain supposed shorthand
signs in the text wholly wrong. On closer
inspection these signs in fact turned out to
places where the ink had cracked and peeled
off the vellum. Newbold's claims were completely demolished.

Since then, many people have tried and failed
to decipher the Voynich manuscript. Some
have proved that it must be a herbal and even
demonstrated some of the lotions and potions
contained inside. But they have not been able
to explain how they cracked their code so their
efforts have been dismissed. Another group of
experts suggested that the manuscript was in
fact in an artificial language, then turned into
code. The question remains – why would
Roger Bacon, a thirteenth-century monk, go to
such great lengths to conceal the meaning of
his work? Even if he did have something to
hide, surely a simple code would have suf-
ficed? The only possible reason for taking such
trouble would be to hide his secret herbal
recipes from his rivals. In which case, he won!

And so the mystery of the Voynich manuscript remains intact, while the manuscript itself lies in Yale University, USA, waiting for someone to decode it. And there it may stay. After all, we don't know who wrote the manuscript, when it was written nor what it said. Not much to go on, is it?

WHO WROTE THE DEAD SEA SCROLLS?

One day in 1947, a young Bedouin boy, Muhammad adh-Dhib was searching for a stray goat in the stretch of desert at the north-western corner of the Dead Sea, when something caught his eye – a narrow, slit-like opening in the rocky cliff below him. Rather absent-mindedly, he threw a couple of pebbles down into the gap . . . and heard the sound of something breaking far below.

Thinking that he might have stumbled across a horde of buried treasure, Muhammad quickly caught up with the goat and headed home. Later he returned to the spot, with a friend, to see if his suspicions were true. The boys squeezed through the opening and found themselves standing in a small, stuffy cave. In it, among a mass of broken pottery pieces they found several long clay cylinders.

In great excitement, the boys pulled off the lids and peered inside, their excitement quickly turning to disappointment. For instead of precious gold and jewels, all the cylinders contained were some dark, musty lumps wrapped up in linen cloth. They turned out to be eleven scrolls, made of sheepskin strips stitched together and covered in sticky, rotting leather. The scrolls ranged in length from one to eight metres. On one side, they were inscribed in what looked like an ancient version of the Hebrew script. They were not quite what the boys had expected, nor hoped for. Even so, they gathered them up and sold them to a dealer in Jerusalem. They didn't get very much for them but it was better than nothing.

Unbeknown to them, and quite by accident, the two boys had stumbled across some of the most important manuscripts ever discovered – the Dead Sea Scrolls. But they were not the only ones who did not appreciate the enormity of the find. A member of the Department of Antiquities in Palestine examined the scrolls and announced them "worthless". The following year, however, five of the scrolls were bought by the Syrian Orthodox Monastery of

St Mark for a staggering sum of £90,000. The six remaining scrolls were bought by the Hebrew University in Jerusalem. It was fast becoming clear that they were anything but worthless.

The scrolls bought by the Monastery of St Mark were examined by an eminent historian, Dr John Trever, the director of the American School of Oriental Research in Jerusalem. He found that one of the scrolls contained the Old Testament book of Isaiah. And the type and form of the Hebrew writing used suggested that the scrolls might date back to before the time of Christ. It was a truly sensational discovery – there was no other book of the Old Testament, written in Hebrew, known to be more than 1,300 years old. According to Dr Trever, the scrolls could predate any known books by almost 700 years. In fact, they were probably even older than that. Historian and archaeologist, Dr William Albright of the Johns Hopkins University, USA, examined photographs of the scrolls and dated them to around 100 BC. It was, he announced, "an absolutely incredible find – the greatest manuscript discovery of modern times".

News of the scrolls spread quickly and soon archaeologists and Bedouin tribesmen were busy exploring more of the region around the

Dead Sea in the hope of striking lucky a second time. Their efforts paid off. By 1956, ten more secret caves were discovered, each containing more pots and more scrolls. As find after find was made, it became clear to the experts that these were not isolated nor accidental hiding places. The scrolls must have formed part of a much larger library which, for some long-lost reason, had been hidden in the desert.

But who had hidden the scrolls in the first place? When archaeologists excavated the area immediately around the cave where the first scrolls were found, they unearthed the ruins of an ancient monastery, called Khirbet Qumran, which had once been the headquarters of an obscure religious sect. In the main building of the monastery they found a writing room, equipped with a pot of dried ink and a clay pot, identical to the clay cylinders found in the first cave. Could the Qumran community have written the scrolls? Had they then hidden them in the nearby caves to prevent them being found and destroyed by the approaching Roman army which invaded the region in AD 68 or AD 70? It seemed very likely. For, in addition to the books of the Old Testament and various commentaries on the books, the scrolls also contain texts which give details of the life, beliefs and disciplines of the Qumran sect. They show the community to have been very similar in its everyday life to a Jewish mystic sect, called the Essenes, which existed between about 125 BC to AD 68. They were celibate and renounced all worldly possessions. The Roman historian, Pliny the Elder, wrote that they had set up their headquarters in the region west of the Dead Sea – exactly where the monastery was discovered. Could the Qumran and Essenes be one and the same?

Most of the scrolls and fragments of text found are in Hebrew. Others are in Aramaic, the language which Christ himself is believed to have spoken. They contain more than five hundred books of writings, including all the books of the Old Testament. The scrolls that document the history of the Qumran community also contain intriguing references which scholars consider to be important links with the earliest beginnings of Christianity. They mention a "Teacher of Righteousness" who seems to have been seen as someone who would prepare the way for the coming of a Messiah. This might be a reference to John the Baptist who travelled far and wide throughout Judaea, preparing the way for

Jesus Christ. Some scholars have even suggested that Jesus himself might have belonged to the Essenes. Is it possible that Christianity began with an obscure sect who lived and died, in an isolated desert retreat? But there the trail goes cold, for the writers of the scrolls do not mention Jesus by name so may not have considered him to be the Messiah.

Scholars all over the world continue to study and debate the authorship and importance of the Dead Sea Scrolls. And controversy continues to follow them. Perhaps one day they will solve this fascinating mystery once and for all . . .

THE GREAT SIBERIAN EXPLOSION
What Caused the Earth to Shake?

One fateful night in June 1908, the world of the people of Nizhne-Karelinsk, a small village in central Siberia, Russia, shook violently and almost literally fell apart. The first they had noticed of the terror to come was a whitish-blue tongue of fire which streaked across the sky. Over the next ten minutes or so, the tongue grew longer and longer until it seemed to be in danger of splitting the sky in two. Then, before the villagers' astonished eyes, the light fell out of the sky and crashed into the ground below where it shattered into a million pieces to create a enormous black cloud of dense, choking smoke. Seconds later, there followed the most tremendous explosion that made the earth shake and every building in the village tremble. Many of the villagers fell to their knees – this truly seemed like the end of the world.

So what *had* caused the "Great Siberian Explosion"? One thing was for certain. Whatever it was, it could have caused far more damage if it had landed in a more heavily populated region. Small comfort for the petrified villagers of Nizhne-Karelinsk. In fact, the village had been some 150 kilometres away from the actual point where the object, whatever it was, had crashed into the earth. Yet the terrible force of the impact had been felt for hundreds of kilometres around. Tiles had been shaken from rooftops; an express train was derailed – the effect was like that of an enormous earthquake.

Whatever it was that had struck Siberia had exploded with a force more powerful than anything ever known before. The shockwaves from the bang travelled around the world before dying out and the vast clouds of dust and gases it poured into the atmosphere had a long-lasting effect on global weather. For most of that extraordinary summer, the sky stayed light well into the night – midnight looked a bright, sunny afternoon. And for many months, the world had breath-taking sunsets and dawns, more spectacular than any seen before. There were only two things which could have caused such disruption to the weather – a violent volcanic explosion or . . . a nuclear reaction. The mystery deepened. The strange thing was that no one at the time seemed very interested in taking the matter further . . .

Thirteen years went by. The First World War was fought and the Russian Revolution toppled the tsar. It was only then that an attempt to unravel the mystery of the explosion was made, and that the matter came to the attention of the general public for the first time. Lenin, the USSR's new leader, wanted his country to stand at the forefront of world science and commissioned some eminent scientists to study, among other things, meteorite falls from outer space. In the course of their research, they came across a few, brief newspaper articles from Siberia which roused their interest and suspicion. It became increasingly

obvious that there was more to the events of
June 1908 than met the eye. For a start, none
of the reports agreed with each other about
what had caused the explosion. Could it have
been a meteorite? It was possible. But the scientists were convinced that it was no ordinary
meteorite.

Eyewitness reports backed them up. People
described how the ground had opened up and
poured a great column of dazzlingly bright
smoke and fire into the air. Many described
being badly burnt, as if by the sun, down one
side of their bodies but not down the other.
Some had suffered temporary deafness – the
noise of the blast had been tremendous; others
were still suffering from shock. Yet, not a single person had been seriously injured or killed.
It was almost unbelievable. By avoiding
crowded cities or even the sea (and the danger
of tidal waves), a catastrophe of unimaginable
proportions had been averted. But the meteorite theory still held sway. A local weatherman
had been able to estimate the actual point of
impact – he was now given official backing to
set out to find it.

The region of Siberia where the explosion
occurred is covered in thick forest – one of the
most inaccessible regions on earth. Whole
areas have never been explored or only sur-

veyed from the air. Weather conditions are incredibly hostile – bitterly cold in winter; boggy and thick with mosquitoes in summer. There are wide rivers to be crossed – but how? The task facing the scientists proved almost impossible before they even set out. Which way should they go? And how should they get there?

In March 1927, the expedition set out. Two local guides who had witnessed the explosion accompanied the scientists. After many setbacks and hardship, they finally arrived at the Mekirta river, close to the point of impact. An astonishing sight met their eyes. On one bank of the river stood thick, untouched forest. On the other, the scene was one of total devastation. For as far as the scientists could see, not a single tree remained standing – the blast had ripped them up by the roots, by the thousand. And this was only a fraction of the total affected area. It was almost too much to take in. The blast must have been far greater than any, even the wildest reports, had given credit for. But the scientists were unable to go any further that day – the guides were frightened. They refused to venture into the devastated forest and the expedition was forced to turn back.

Two months later, the scientists returned,

determined to take matters further. For several days, they followed the line of flattened trees, then pitched camp and began to survey the surrounding countryside. Before very long, they had found what they believed to be the centre of the blast – a vast, scorched circle of earth, surrounded by charred and burnt trees, some of which were, incredibly, still standing. Soon the full horror of the situation became apparent – the blast had flattened some three thousand square kilometres of forest. It was worse than they had ever anticipated. At this point, the scientists still suspected that a meteorite was responsible for the devastation and they began to search for remains. But nothing they found proved conclusive. Several small, water-filled pits *could* have been made by meteorite fragments but not necessarily. It was all very strange.

The scientist leading the expedition, Leonid Kulik, made three further trips to the region. He remained, until his death, convinced that the blast could be blamed on an unusually large meteroite. The only thing he lacked was any evidence to back up his theory. Despite months of searching, he could find no pieces of metal or rock, nor any other fragments of such a meteorite. Indeed, he was never able to prove that any such object had hit the ground

– there was no crater, nothing.

In the following decades, many conflicting theories and finds came to light. The area of devastation was found to be far smaller than first assumed. And at the very point where a crater should have been, the trees were still standing. Eyewitnesses reported seeing the object swerve off course before it hit the ground, not something a meteorite would ever have done. More curiously, trees that had survived the blast either stopped growing altogether or shot up far more quickly than normal. New species of insects began to appear in the blast region. None of this suggested a gigantic meteorite. Rather it suggested a gigantic bomb. Soon similarities were being drawn between aspects of this blast and that of the nuclear bombs which had devastated the Japanese cities of Hiroshima and Nagasaki at the end of the Second World War.

It seemed far-fetched but could it be true? It certainly would explain the absence of a crater, the burns which people suffered (now known to be caused by radiation) and the puzzling changes to the region's plants and animals. All these things were found to occur in Japan. A mushroom-shaped cloud had accompanied the blast. But one crucial piece of evidence was missing. When the region's radiation levels were tested, they were found to be perfectly normal!

And so the mystery, and the controversy, of the Great Siberian Explosion continues. It has even been suggested that an alien space ship was to blame for the blast, having veered off course and into the earth where its nuclear reactors had exploded. Another theory was that a black hole was responsible. Or was the explosion caused by a build up of anti-matter which had exploded on contact with the earth? Had the earth been hit by a gigantic comet? If so, how had it managed to approach the earth without being tracked by astronomers as comets normally are? Besides, none of the observatories questioned by the experts had any record of such a thing. Almost a century after it took place, it looks highly unlikely that the cause of the explosion which shook Siberia will ever be discovered.

UNIDENTIFIED FLYING OBJECTS

UFOs — FACT OR FICTION?

Unidentified Flying Objects — UFOs, for short — have been sighted all over the world, by all sorts of people, ranging from astronauts and aircraft pilots to farmers and policeman. These mysterious objects have been photographed and filmed (though many of the photographs have later been dismissed as fakes); hundreds of books and articles have been written about them; whole magazines are dedicated to them and international conferences are held to discuss them. But what are they and where do they come from? Do they, in fact, exist at all, or are they simply figments of people's imaginations?

All kinds of suggestions have been put forward to account for the sudden and strange appearance of bright lights, flying saucers, glowing blobs and mysterious craft of every shape and size in the sky. They tend to appear in rural areas rather than cities, at twilight, either in the early morning or evening. Most have been seen by people on the ground, though several famous examples have been spotted by astronauts and aircraft pilots from the air. Many UFO sightings may never have been reported at all, for fear of ridicule. So what are they? Could they be plane lights, or satellites, fireballs, or the effect of the sun shining through the clouds, as many cynics claim them to be? Or could they really be alien spacecraft surveying the Earth, for which we have no logical explanation? Ufologists, people who study UFOs, are in no doubt that the latter theory is the correct one. What do you think? Have you ever seen, or thought you saw, a UFO? Did you tell anyone? Did they *believe* you? If you have sighted a UFO, you are NOT ALONE! Feast your eyes on some of the world's greatest UFO mysteries, and make your own mind up!

THE UFO CASEBOOK

Early sightings

• Incredible though it seems, reports of UFOs go right back to Biblical times. The following account appears in the Old Testament, of an extraordinary spectacle seen by the prophet, Ezekiel:

"Behold, a whirlwind came out of the north, a great cloud, a fire enfolding it. A great brightness, the colour of amber, shone from the midst of the fire. Also out of the midst came four living creatures. This is what they looked like. Each one looked like a man, and each one had four faces, and each one had four wings. And their legs were straight; they had hooves like cows and they sparkled like the colour of burnished brass. Under their wings, they had human hands. Each of their four faces were turned to the four quarters."

It was later discovered that these extraordinary apparitions must have arisen because of a rare atmospheric effect, where the onlooker sees four "sundogs" spaced evenly in a ring around the sun. But you never know . . .

• The Roman historian, Livy, writing in the first centuries BC and AD, seems to have been a keen early ufologist. He recorded about thirty strange objects which had been sighted in the sky, not by him, it has to be said, but by earlier observers. Among these accounts, he describes how a group of spaceships was seen in 218 BC and a group of men dressed in white, gathered around an altar, in 214 BC. Livy had no doubt that these must have

been creatures from outer space.

• On the evening of New Year's Day 1254, a group of monks in St Albans, England, claimed to have seen "a kind of large ship, elegantly shaped, and well equipped and of marvellous colour" in the night sky. In 1290, another group of monks at Byland Abbey in Yorkshire, England, witnessed "a large round silver disc fly slowly over them".

Unidentified Flying Cigars?

• On the night of 21 April 1897, Mr Alexander Hamilton, a respectable member of the US House of Representatives, was woken up by a strange spacecraft which appeared to be coming down to land outside his farm. In a sworn statement, he described the craft as consisting of "a great cigar-shaped portion, possibly three hundred feet long, with a carriage underneath".

He went on to report that the "carriage" was made of a shiny substance like glass, and metal, though he could not identify what sort of metal it was. The craft was brilliantly lit and he could see the inside of the spacecraft quite clearly — it was occupied by "six of the strangest beings I ever saw. They were jabbering together, but I could not understand a word they said." As soon as Mr Hamilton and two of his farm-workers moved into the open for a closer inspection, the spacecraft, and its amazing alien crew, soared away, never to be seen again. Although many people dismissed his account as nonsense, Mr Hamilton refused to take back a single word of his statement. He was convinced of what he had seen . . .

• Hundreds of other cigar-shaped spacecraft have since been reported. In 1909, in Wales, a cylindrical spaceship was witnessed landing on a road. Two beings, dressed in fur coats, got out and began speaking quickly and excitedly in a bizarre, unknown language. When they realized that they were being watched, they returned to their spacecraft and took off again.

The Flying Saucer Story

• The term "flying saucer" was coined in June 1947, when an American pilot, Kenneth Arnold, who was taking part in a search for a missing aircraft, spotted nine, gleaming disc-shaped objects flying over the Cascade Mountains, Washington, USA. He said later that the objects flew in much the same way as a saucer would if you skimmed it across the water.

Arnold was a fire appliance salesman by trade. He was also an experienced and trusted pilot who was sometimes hired to take part in rescue
missions. No one had any reason at
all to doubt that he was telling the
truth. Soon his sensational tale was
being splashed all over the national
and international newspapers, and the
mysterious objects were labelled
"flying saucers".

On the afternoon of 24 June 1947,
Arnold had taken off from Chehalis
Airport, Washington to search for a
transport plane which had crashed
somewhere in the mountains. A reward
of $5,000 was being offered to anyone
who could find the plane, and Arnold
was determined to claim the money.
The day was clear and bright. As he
circled over the area where the lost
plane had last been sighted, a flash
of light caught his eye. At first he
thought it must be another aircraft,
perhaps also involved in the search.
Then, as he glanced north across the
mountains, he saw something much more
unusual coming out of the sky. In his

book about the event, entitled *The Coming of the Saucers*, he says:

"*I observed far to my left and to the north a formation of nine very bright objects coming from the vicinity of Mount Baker, flying very close to the mountain tops and travelling at tremendous speed. I could see no tails on them and they flew like no aircraft I had ever seen before*".

The nine aircraft were flying in a long line at an altitude of about 2,800 metres. Every few seconds, two or three of the spaceships would change course slightly, tilting and dipping, so that their shiny surfaces glinted in the light of the sun. They were about the size of ordinary passenger aircraft, but were round, with no visible tail surfaces. More extraordinary still, when Arnold tried to estimate their speed by timing how quickly they flew from one mountain top to another, he was astonished to discover that the "flying saucers" were travelling at about 1,700 kilometres-per-hour, a speed undreamt of for any aircraft in 1947! When the objects finally flew away, Arnold, all thought of the missing plane long gone from his mind, turned his own plane round and headed back to base.

When he landed, he decided to report what he had seen to the FBI but their office was closed. Instead, he went straight to the press. UFO fever had begun! Within a few hours, the newspaper offices were swamped with calls from other people who claimed to have seen similar saucer-shaped craft. Arnold found himself at the centre of a hysterical media frenzy. Later, he said:

"From then on, if I was to go by the number of reports that came in from the sightings, of which I kept a close track, I thought it wouldn't be long before there would be one of these things in every garage. In order to stop what I thought was a lot of foolishness, and since I couldn't get any work done, I went out to the airport, cranked up my plane, and flew home . . ."

• Arnold's tale sparked off a whole range of other flying saucer sightings both in the Washington mountains and abroad but these were dismissed by the authorities as hallucinations. The editor of the magazine, *Flying Saucer Review*, was dubious. For such a large number of people to suffer from the *same* hallucination was surely beyond the bounds of medical probability, he said!

• In January 1948, an American airman disappeared as he flew to investigate an "unidentified object" in Kentucky. The object was described as "metallic" and "tremendous in size". The US Air Force refused to accept the popular view that he had been shot down by a flying saucer. It claimed instead that what the airman had mistaken for a flying saucer was in fact the planet Venus.

• By 1966, a poll revealed that a staggering five million Americans claimed to have seen a flying saucer of some description. Some had undoubtedly seen perfectly harmless weather ballooons, aircraft lights or unusual cloud formations, and let their imaginations do the rest. But surely they couldn't *all* be wrong?

UFOs in Outer Space
• Although many UFOs are spotted from the ground, there are several amazing

instances of astronauts spying alien craft whilst in orbit in outer space. And, however extraordinary these may seem, they surely cannot be totally dismissed. After all, astronauts are highly trained professionals – it seems unlikely that they could simply be "seeing things". One of the most spectacular UFO reports was made by two US *Gemini 4* astronauts, James McDivitt and Ed White, in June 1965. As they orbited the Earth some 120 kilometres above the surface of the Pacific Ocean, they saw a strange, metallic, cylindrical-shaped object, which seemed to have long arms or projections sticking out of it. The two men assumed that the object must be an unidentified spacecraft, and the arms must be antennae. McDivitt grabbed his cine-camera and took some film of the spacecraft and several still photographs. When these were later developed, they showed a hazy object outlined against the sky. But the photographs were never released for the public to see.

Suddenly, McDivitt and White noticed something very strange about the spacecraft's course. It had been following a path roughly parallel to the *Gemini 4* capsule. Now, however, it appeared to be closing in fast. Then, as the astronauts prepared to take evasive action, the UFO disappeared from sight.

At first, McDivitt thought that he must have seen, and filmed, an unmanned satellite which had somehow strayed off course. And this is what the US authorities encouraged people to believe. The official US Air Force

explanation was that the astronauts had seen the unmanned photographic satellite, *Pegasus*. This was equipped with long, protuding "arms" to register hits from meteorites. What they could not explain, however, was the fact that this particular satellite was some 1,600 kilometres away at the time of McDivitt's sighting.

• Since spaceflight began, UFOs have been sighted by at least thirty astronauts. On 15 May 1963, a Mercury capsule blasted into space from Cape Canaveral to begin a 22-orbit journey around the world. On board was Major Gordon Cooper, an extremely experienced pilot and astronaut. As he orbited the Earth for the final time, he reported seeing something odd in the sky. Ahead he could see a green, glowing object, and it was coming straight towards him. The nearest tracking station, at Perth, Australia, also picked up the object on their radar screen. When Cooper landed, a crowd of reporters was waiting to interview him – news of his sighting had been rapidly relayed

around the world. They were told, however, that they would not be allowed
to ask him any questions about the
incident. The official line was that
Cooper had been hallucinating because
of an accidental release of carbon
monoxide gas into his helmet on his
last-but-one orbit. Cooper himself was
having none of it. He was convinced
that he had indeed seen a UFO and
remained a firm believer throughout
the rest of his career.

• When, on 20 July 1969, the American
astronaut Neil Armstrong took his
"one small step for man, one giant
leap for mankind" and became the
first person to walk on the moon, he
claimed he was being watched. As he
stepped out of his *Apollo II* spacecraft, he spotted two UFOs on the rim
of a nearby crater. Back in the
spacecraft, he reported his sighting
to mission control in Houston, while
his co-pilot, Buzz Aldrin, filmed the
alien spaceships.

This was the claim made by Maurice
Chatelain, a member of the National
Aeronautics and Space Administration

team at the time of Armstrong's historic mission. But, Chatelain alleged, NASA ordered the incident to be covered up and Armstrong's reports were blacked out from the broadcasts which went round the world "for security reasons".

NASA, in turn, dismissed the whole story as ridiculous, claiming that the only conversations kept from the public were private discussions between the astronauts and their doctors. But the Russian space expert Professor Sergei Boshich added his support for the UFO sighting.

"It is my opinion," he said, "that beings from another civilization picked up radio signals from Earth and spied on the Apollo landing to learn the extent of our knowledge. Then they took off without making contact."

• In June 1980, UFO hysteria gripped the former Soviet Union as hundreds of thousands of people witnesssed a massive, crescent-shaped spacecraft streaking across the Russian skies. The mysterious object glowed bright red. Panic broke out. Some people thought that Russia was about to be invaded by aliens from outer space – reports even reached the press of aliens being seen on the streets of Moscow and other major Russian cities. Other people believed that the country was being attacked by American nuclear weapons. The strange object was also seen in various parts of South America, including Chile, Brazil, Uruguay and Argentina. Mysteriously it was, by now, much smaller in size and glowed much less brightly than before. In the end, the mystery was solved by the US Air Defense Command which had been tracking the object by radar.

But this was one UFO which could be identified – it was, in fact, a booster rocket used to launch one of Russia's military satellites. The glow was caused as the rocket burned up on re-entering the Earth's atmosphere. This particular panic was over!

Close Encounters . . .

• What began for police patrolman Lonnie Zamora as an ordinary car chase, ended as an extraordinary brush with creatures from another planet. The date was 24 April 1964; the place, Socorro, New Mexico, USA. Patrolman Zamora was chasing a speeding motorist when he caught sight of an amazing spaceship, coming in to land two kilometres away. He gave up the chase and turned his attention instead to the UFO, for that was what he took it to be. Later, when he filed his report, he described how he had found the spaceship on the outskirts of the town. It was about the size of a car, oval-shaped and made of some unknown shiny metal. And standing beside it, he continued, were two strange humanoid figures, about the size of ten-year-old children. But as patrolman Zamora returned to his car to report his findings, the two figures got back into their spaceship and sped off into the sky. All that was left to show of their brief visit to Earth was a small, circular crater in the ground . . .

• A year later, in southern France, a lavender farmer saw two tiny figures in his field. They were standing next to an object "about the size of a Renault car". Thinking they were local boys trying to steal his precious crop, he ran towards them, intending chase them off. When he was almost upon them, one of the figures turned towards him and pointed a strange-looking instrument at him. The farmer claimed that the instrument's beam left him paralysed, and the two figures got into their car-like craft and took off.

Was this just another in a long list of UFO sightings? It certainly seemed so, at first, and no one thought any more of it. But then the story took a stranger turn. Some time later, the lavender farmer was shown a photograph – it showed a model based on patrolman Zamora's description of the UFO seen in New Mexico the year before. The farmer seemed to recognize the spaceship and fell into a state of deep shock from which it took him some time to recover. Could the two men have seen the same spacecraft? Where would it turn up next?

• At dawn on 24 October 1967, two police constables in Devon, England, were involved in a high-speed chase with a mysterious object which looked like a gigantic, shining cross. The chase went

on for almost an hour. At a press conference after the event, the two men
said that the object looked like "a
star-spangled cross, radiating points of
light from all angles". One of them
added, "It seemed to be watching us and
would not let us catch up. It . . . knew we
were chasing it."

The British Ministry of Defence
claimed that the strange object was in
fact a giant jet tanker belonging to the
US Air Force which was on a refuelling
mission. According to other reports,
however, none of these jet tankers were
in the air at that time.

The Daily Mystery

Mississippi, USA

12 October 1973

WE WERE ABDUCTED BY ALIENS

Aliens took our photos, men claim

Two Mississippi shipyard workers claim to have been taken on board a spaceship and examined by aliens, our reporter was told yesterday.

The two men, Charles Hickson, aged 42, and Calvin Parker, aged 19, were out fishing when the incident occurred.

"It was terrible," Mr Hickson told our reporter.

The two men claimed to

have been taken aboard an egg-shaped UFO which came out of the skies and hovered a metre or so above the river. Once on board, they were given a thorough examination by three humanoid creatures. Mr Hickson said the creatures kept them there for about twenty minutes.

"Then they took our photos," he added, "and let us go."

His companion, Mr Parker, said that when he first saw the bizarre creatures, he was so frightened, he fainted.

"They weren't like any creatures I've ever seen before," he said. "They had silvery skin and no eyes. They had slits for their mouths, and three points on their faces where their ears and nose should have been."

After their ordeal, the two men were interviewed by Dr J. Allen Hynek, a well-known astronomer and the US Air Force's chief investigator of UFOs. They have also agreed to being questioned under hypnosis at some later date, to prove the truth of their story.

When we asked Dr Hynek his opinion of the men's experiences, this is what he told us:

"They had undergone such a shocking thing that they couldn't put it exactly into words. Whatever happened to them definitely affected their rationality."

Bird's eye view

• A large number of suspected UFOs have been sighted by airline pilots. Many more may have gone unreported so that the pilots do not end up being branded as cranks! Most of these reports concern mysterious craft which perform manoeuvres and fly at speeds which no ordinary aircraft could match. Then they disappear. Sometimes the watching aircraft disappears too . . .

In 1953, two US Air Force pilots in an F-89 jet chased a UFO as it sped across Lake Superior on the border between Canada and the USA. Their movements were tracked by radar. Suddenly, the radar screen showed the two craft, known and unknown, merge together. Then the jet vanished and the UFO passed out of the radar's range. Although a thorough search was mounted, by air and sea, no trace was ever found of the jet or its two pilots.

• During World War II, there were a great many reports of mysterious balls of light flying alongside

Allied planes as they embarked on bombing raids over Germany. A name was even coined for them — "Foo Fighters". The Allied airmen presumed they must be German in origin. A newspaper report, dating from December 1944, describes them as the Germans' latest secret weapons — "mysterious silvery balls which float in the air". But the German pilots had experienced similar encounters and thought, in turn, that the strange objects must be British or American.

It was widely believed by ufologists that the Foo Fighters were robots sent out from an alien mother ship to gather information about the Earth and its fighting machines, before an invasion could be attempted. The real explanation is equally mysterious, however. The balls of light were in fact examples of ball lightning, about 25 centimetres across and glowing orange or red. The lightning appears suddenly from clouds or from a clear sky and lasts for only a minute or two before vanishing. Some of the balls explode with a bang; others simply fade into the air. Ball lightning is a very odd scientific phenomenon, still little understood. The balls seem to search out the insides of things, such as buildings or vehicles. Sometimes they hiss or crackle, or give off a smell like bad eggs — the UFOs of the natural world.

• In the early morning of 6 December 1952, Lieutenant Sid Coleman was watching the radar screen of his B-29 bomber as he flew over the Gulf of Mexico. Suddenly, a blip appeared on the screen, closely followed by two other blips. The blips were not like any other objects Lieutenant Coleman had ever seen before. Moreover, the mysterious craft were travelling at an astonishing 8,400 km/h. Meanwhile, another four blips had appeared on the navigator's radar.

With one blip fast approaching from the right, another member of the bomber's crew, Master Sergeant Bailey, strained his eyes to see in the twilight sky. He watched in amazement as a streak of blue light flashed along the length of the plane. By now, many more blips were appearing thick and fast on the plane's radar. The bomber seemed to be surrounded on all sides. Up in the cockpit, Captain John Harter saw the UFOs cut straight across the B-29's course. Then, suddenly, they turned and headed straight towards the bomber. As they approached, they slowed down to the bomber's speed and shadowed it for about ten seconds – it seemed that they were playing some bizarre game of cat and mouse with the plane. Then, before the bomber crew's astonished eyes, the smaller UFOs speeded up and merged into a larger craft, before accelerating away at incredible speeds of over 14,000 km/h.

What had the bomber crew seen that morning? The fact that the UFOs could be tracked by radar seemed to show that they were solid objects, and therefore real. The crew could also back up the radar with the evidence of their own eyes. One explanation was that the objects must have been missiles or jet aircraft. In 1952,

the Korean War was in full swing and
the US Air Force was conducting a
large number of test flights and
missile tests at that time. These
aircraft would have been fast and
high-flying, with clusters of navigation lights which could easily be
mistaken for something more mysterious. Many reports of UFOs tell of
flashing green, white and red lights,
all of which could be explained by
the different coloured navigation
lights on a jet.

However, things are not always as
clear-cut as they first appear and,
tempting though these explanations
seem, the people who have actually
witnessed UFOs take a lot more convincing.

• In 1988, the pilot and crew of a
Japanese Airlines plane twice reported seeing a gigantic UFO, shaped like
a walnut, in the skies. In January
1988, the Boeing 747 en route from
Iceland to Japan was shadowed by the
strange object for about thirty minutes as it flew over Alaska, USA. The
captain, Kenju Terauchi, described

the mysterious craft as "very big, about twice the size of an aircraft carrier". When the object began to close in on the aircraft, Captain Terauchi radioed air-traffic control and asked permission to take avoiding action, if necessary. Permission was granted — the object had also appeared on the controllers' radar screen. Like Captain Terauchi, they had no idea what it was, but it looked as if it could be made up of three smaller craft flying close together. An official investigation was launched, but no conclusions were ever reached.

Lights over Wanaque

The night of 11 January 1966 began as any other for Patrolman George Dykman. It was bitterly cold. Dykman pulled his coat tightly around him and shivered as he gazed out over the expanse of Wanaque Reservoir, New Jersey, USA. Despite the cold, the frozen reservoir looked serene and peaceful as it lay glittering and glinting under the light of the beautifully clear stars.

The peaceful scene was short-lived. Out of the corner of his eye, Dykman suddenly spotted an unknown object flying very slowly over the northern end of the reservoir. At first, he thought it must be an aircraft, perhaps flying off course. But his astonishment grew as he watched the object grow bigger, then transform itself into a brilliant white ball of light. The longer Dykman looked, the more extraordinary the scene became. From brilliant white, the light turned red, then green, then back to white again. Dykman began to grow seriously alarmed. This was not a situation he could deal with on his own. He rushed back to his patrol car and radioed a warning to other patrol cars known to be in the vicinity. Within a few minutes, several of his colleagues had arrived on the scene and joined Dykman as he gazed in amazement at the shining object, which was still hovering above the frozen reservoir.

Patrolman Dykman and his colleagues were not the only people to witness this strange sight. Other people had seen it too, among them the Mayor of Wanaque and his 14-year-old son. A crowd of curious onlookers quickly gathered on the banks of the reservoir. By now, the UFO, if that is indeed what it was, was shining with a red light and cruising backwards and forwards in a strange swinging movement across the ice. It seemed to be about 3 metres wide.

Suddenly, the craft climbed into the air and stopped still. A brilliant beam of light, like an extremely powerful spotlight, shone down from it on to the watchers by the reservoir. For the next hour, the light flashed on and off as if it were trying to send some sort of message. What that message was, no one knew. Then, as suddenly as it had appeared, the object began to climb steeply and accelerate away at great speed. Soon, it was lost from view among the night sky. The excited crowd began to disperse – the discussions about what they had seen would last long into the night. Their place was taken by scores of newspaper reporters and photographers, all desperate for the scoop of the century. They were to be deeply disappointed. When nothing unusual had appeared for two hours or more, they packed up their gear and headed back home. Two policemen were left to keep watch. Thirty minutes later, at about 2 a.m., the mysterious light returned. As the two policemen watched through their binoculars, they noticed that the object looked different this time – like a cluster of brilliant stars. After a few minutes, it once again vanished from view.

Next morning, reservoir officials went out to inspect the ice at the northern end of the reservoir – the very spot over which the UFO had been hovering. Here they found a series of almost circular holes in the ice, through which the water was welling up. It was as if the holes had been melted in the ice by a number of giant blow-torches . . .

Over the next few nights, further mysteriously glowing objects were sighted in the skies over Wanaque. They were oval-shaped or circular, and ranged in colour from brilliant white to bright blue. The following spring, a UFO flew low over a convent just outside Wanaque, terrifying the nuns who lived there. Several more UFOs appeared during the summer. But the next major sighting did not occur until October when once again, the Wanaque Reservoir became the focus of the town's attention. On 12 October, a "flying saucer" was seen hovering above the reservoir. This time it came down low enough over the water to stir the surface up into waves. Before very long, the Wanaque UFO was once again splashed over every newspaper in America.

While many of the people of Wanaque were convinced that they had seen a genuine UFO, others were not so sure. A great number of weird and wonderful theories began to circulate to account for the spacecraft. One theory was that there was a UFO base hidden deep beneath the waters of the reservoir. Another, even more fantastic suggestion was that UFOs were being sent to every reservoir in the world in order to drug the water (and the people who drank it) so that invaders from outer space could land and take over the Earth! The first official explanation, issued by the Air Force, was that the mysterious craft were nothing stranger than brightly-lit helicopters. The second, issued just a few days later, was that the lights were in fact the planet Venus! To the people who had witnessed the UFOs, including Patrolman Dykman, neither explanation rang true. After all, how could the planet Venus possibly get close enough to stir up the waters of a reservoir?

Bogus UFOs

• But beware! For every allegedly "true" sighting of an alien or UFO, there are several hoaxes to be dismissed and discounted. The problem is that it is often very difficult to tell the two apart!

• In 1975, two American tricksters, Marshall Herff Applewhite and Bonnie Lu Trusdale Nettles, commonly known as "Bo" and "Peep", announced to the world that they had come to this planet by UFO from "the level above human". Their mission was to enlist as many humans as possible in a mysterious project called the "Process" and take them back to the higher level they themselves had come from. The only thing people had to do to take part in the Process was to hand over all their valuables and possessions! As proof that they were telling the truth, Bo and Peep declared that, within six months, their physical bodies would be killed off and that their spirits would guide the new recruits to their new lives in the sky. Incredibly, about a thousand people fell for their scheme, although numbers did drop off when the promised assassinations failed to happen!

Alien communications

• Ever since Kenneth Arnold's sighting of a flying saucer (see page 221), people have come forward claiming to have been abducted or kid-

napped by aliens and taken aboard
their spaceships. Some of these incidents are dealt with above (see page
234). Another short selection follows
here.

• One of the most extraordinary
abduction claims turned out to be an
elaborate hoax. In a book entitled,
Flying Saucers Have Landed, an
American hamburger salesman, George
Adamski, claimed not only to have
seen UFOs but to have been carried
off by one. Adamski wrote that, while
he and several other flying saucer
enthusiasts were driving through the
Californian desert in 1952 to investigate a suspected landing site, they
saw an enormous cigar-shaped object
in the sky. Adamski stopped the car
and wandered off alone, with his camera. Up ahead, he saw, he says, a
flying saucer come in to land on the
barren desert ground. Adamski hurried
towards the saucer where he met a
small man with long blond hair, who
used sign language to communicate
that he came from the planet Venus.
Then he flew off in his spacecraft.

The meeting had been witnessed, from a distance, by Adamski's friends and they later signed statements verifying what they had seen.

In his second book, *Inside the Space Ships*, Adamski describes another encounter with an alien craft. This time he tells how he was taken for several rides in a flying saucer, called a "scout ship", by the man from Venus whom he had met earlier, and two other men, one from Mars and the other from Saturn. On the first trip, Adamski was taken to the mother ship. On the second, he was taken to the far side of the moon, which was being used as a base by the aliens. Here he saw various four-legged animals and lush vegetation, including trees. He was also shown pictures of Venus and reported that they showed rivers, mountains and large cities – in fact, the planet was an ideal place to live on, by all accounts. Even when faced with overwhelming evidence to the contrary – in 1962, the space probe *Mariner II*, flew past Venus and sent back pictures of its unbreathable sulphuric gas atmosphere

— Adamski refused to change a word of his story. He said that he much preferred to rely on first-hand evidence from a real-life Venusian, than on a man-made space probe. He spent the last years of his life lecturing about his experiences and died in 1965, four years before the first men landed on the moon and revealed that, in reality, it was a dry, dusty place where nothing could grow.

Despite everything, however, Adamski's two books were best-sellers . . .

• Late in the evening of 21 August 1955, young Billy Sutton stepped outside his father's farmhouse in Kentucky, USA, to get a drink of water from the well. Suddenly, he noticed a shining, round object. It hovered over the farm, then dropped out of sight. Billy ran back inside and told his father what he had seen.

"It's nothing," replied Elmer Sutton. "Just some shooting star, or something. It's that time of year."

With that the matter was dropped until, an hour or so later, the farm dogs began to bark furiously — a sure sign that there was a intruder outside in the yard. Elmer and his eldest son, John, went outside to investigate. Nothing in their lives could have prepared them for what they saw next.

A few metres away from the farmhouse, there stood the strangest creature they had ever seen. It looked like a small boy, just over a metre tall and it shone with an eerie glow. It seemed to be dressed in a suit of some unknown shiny material. Slowly, and to the Suttons' horror, the creature began to move towards them, half-crouching, half-running, like a large ape. As it came closer, the terrified family could make out more of its features — it had a large, egg-shaped head which looked far too big for its small body and very long arms, with webbed hands and gleaming, claw-like talons. When it was almost upon them, the creature stopped and stared at them. Elmer Sutton grabbed his shotgun, loaded it and fired it straight at the alien. The creature collapsed on the ground.

Thinking it was dead, the Suttons crept towards it for a closer look. The creature stirred . . . then, all of a sudden, it leapt to its feet and ran off into the darkness. The Suttons were petrified. They ran back into the farmhouse, bolted the door and huddled together for safety.

Suddenly, one of the Suttons' daughters shrieked with fright. There, through the open door of the dining room, she could see the creature, standing outside the window. Elmer and John Sutton took up their guns again and fired at the creature through the glass pane. Once again, it vanished into the darkness. Once again, everything was quiet. The Suttons waited . . . and watched.

Then, just as they thought their ordeal was over, the dogs began barking again. Elmer and John picked up their guns, plucked up their courage and went outside. The dogs were standing in a circle around a tree trunk in the yard, barking ferociously. And there, clinging to the tree branches, sat the alien creature itself. Suddenly John shouted to his father – there, behind them, was another alien, crawling along the farmhouse roof. Elmer took aim and fired . . . The creature fell off the roof with a thud and ran away but it appeared to be uninjured – the bullets simply bounced off its shiny skin. Meanwhile, the other alien had climbed down from the tree and dashed off into the undergrowth.

For the next few hours, everything was quiet. There was no further sign of the aliens and the Suttons, at last, began to feel that their terri-fying experience might be at an end. Elmer immediately loaded his family into his station wagon and drove them to the sheriff's office to report what had happened to them. But when the sheriff went back to the farm-house with them to see the scene for himself, all the evidence he could find was a broken window and a few bullet holes in the walls – nothing that hinted in any way at aliens from outer space.

No one knows what the Suttons real-ly saw on that August night. Whatever it was left them utterly terrified.

Could it be that the aliens they saw are out there still, waiting for another chance to strike? Unlikely, but not impossible . . .

• Another couple who claimed to have been abducted by aliens was Barney and Betty Hill of New Hampshire. USA. One night in September 1961, as the Hills were driving home after a trip to Niagara Falls, a bright object appeared from the sky and hovered about the road. As it drew closer to the Hills' car, they could see a row of windows along the object's side, through which several uniformed figures were clearly visible. When the Hills finally reached home some time later, shaken and confused by what they had seen on the road, they found, to their puzzlement, that the two or so hours after the sighting were a total blank. They could remember absolutely nothing about that time at all nor about how they had arrived home.

Soon afterwards, Betty Hill began having nightmares in which she was abducted by aliens and subjected to a gruelling and unpleasant medical examination. Both she and her husband became increasingly nervy and anxious but they had no idea what was causing their problems. Everything had been fine before that fateful night. In an attempt to solve the mystery, they made an appointment to see leading Boston psychiatrist, Dr Benjamin Simon. Under hypnosis, he questioned them closely about their experiences. The story they told him was both astonishing and terrifying. Though questioned separately, both Barney and Betty related the same version of what had happened, right down to the fine details. They told Dr Simon how they had been taken on board the bright object, which had indeed been an alien spacecraft, by men with slanting, cat-like eyes and grey skin who had subjected the Hills to a series of painful and traumatic physical examinations. The aliens took shavings of their skin and nails, and a needle was inserted into Betty Hill's navel. Then they were hypnotized and told to forget everything they had seen or heard.

The only conclusion Dr Simon could reach was that the Hills were telling the truth . . .

There have been many attempts to explain away UFOs as odd-shaped clouds, unusual weather phenomena, brightly-lit aircraft, stray satellites, and even the planet Venus. In many cases, there does seem to be a perfectly rational and reasonable explanation behind a sighting — as in the story about the Foo Fighters, for example. In many cases, however, no such explanation can be found. As far as evidence is concerned, apart from eyewitness statements, a number of photographs have been produced, claiming to be of UFOs. Are they real or are they fake? A large percentage have been proved, scientifically, to be fakes. Some have been tricks of the light or double exposures. Some have been deliberate hoaxes. But others have passed virtually all of the tests carried out on them. So, are they genuine or were those particular photographers simply more ingenious than the others?

Whatever the fact or fiction behind UFOs, one thing is sure – no one knows for certain. Just because we have no hard evidence for the existence of creatures from other planets, does it necessarily follow that they don't exist?

The Battalion that Vanished

In many cases where people have allegedly been abducted by UFOs, the unfortunate victims are usually returned to Earth where they are able to tell others about their ordeal. Whether anyone believes them or not is another matter. Occasionally, however, the victim disappears for ever, never to be seen of or heard from again. Even for one person to vanish in this way is rare. For a whole regiment to disappear is unheard of . . . almost. For this is precisely what happened to an entire battalion of the Royal Norfolk Regiment one August day in 1912.

The incident in question is supposed to have taken place during the ill-fated Gallipoli campaign of World War I. According to a statement made by several eyewitnesses, twenty two New Zealand soldiers watched in stunned silence as a large number of British soldiers, later identified as belonging to the Royal Norfolk Regiment, marched straight into a loaf-shaped cloud whch was lying across a dried-up creek. When the last soldier had entered the cloud, it lifted and wafted away. Not a single one of the men was ever seen again. This is what the statement said:

August 21, 1915

The following is an account of the strange incident that happened on the above date, which occurred in the morning during the severest and final period of fighting which took place on Hill 60, Suvla Bay, Anzac. The day broke clear, without a cloud in sight, as any beautiful Mediterranean day could be expected to be. The exception, however, was a number of perhaps six or eight "loaf of bread" shaped clouds – all shaped exactly alike – which were hovering over Hill 60. It was noticed that, in spite of a 4-5 mph breeze from the south, these clouds did not alter their position in any shape or form, nor did they drift away under the influence of the breeze. They were hovering at an elevation of about 60 degrees as seen from our observation point 500 feet up. Also stationary and resting on the ground right underneath this group of clouds was a similar cloud in shape, measuring about 800 feet in length, 220 feet in height, and 200 feet in width. This cloud was absolutely dense, solid looking in structure . . . . All this was observed by twenty two men of No 3 Section, No 1 Field Company, NZE, including myself, from our trenches on Rhododendron Spur, approximately 2500 yards south-west of the cloud on the ground. Our vantage point was overlooking Hill 60 by about 3000 feet. As it turned out later, this singular cloud was straddling a dry creek bed or sunken road and we had a perfect view of the cloud's sides and ends as it rested on the ground. The colour was light grey, as was the colour of the other clouds. A British Regiment . . . of several hundred men, was then noticed marching up this sunken road or creek towards Hill 60. However, when they arrived at this cloud, they marched straight into it, with no hesitation, but no one ever came out to deploy and fight at Hill 60. About an hour later, after the last of the file had disappeared into it, this cloud very unobtrusively lifted off the ground and, like any cloud or fog would, rose slowly until it joined the other similar clouds which were mentioned at the beginning of this account. On viewing them again, they all looked alike "as peas in a pod". All this time, the group of clouds had been hovering in the same place, but as soon as the singular cloud had risen to their level, they all moved away northwards . . . In a matter of about three-quarters of an hour they had all disappeared from view.

The regiment mentioned was posted as missing or "wiped out", and on Turkey surrendering in 1918, the first thing Britain demanded of Turkey was the return of the regiment. Turkey replied that she had neither captured this regiment, nor made contact with it, and did not know it existed. A British Regiment in 1914–18 consisted of any number between 800 and 4,000 men. Those who observed this incident vouch for the fact that Turkey never captured that regiment, nor made contact with it.

We, the undersigned, although late in time, this is the 50th Jubilee of the Anzac landing, declare that the above described incident is true in every word.

Signed by witnesses:

4/165 Sapper F. Reichardt,
Matata, Bay of Plenty

13/416 Sapper R. Newnes,
157 King Street, Cambridge

J.L. Newman
75 Freyberg Street, Octumoctai, Tauranga

The statement made by the soldiers who witnessed this extraordinary event does contain some inaccuracies, such as the correct name of the regiment involved. But one historical fact prevents it from being immediately dismissed as a figment of the imagination – a battalion of the Royal Norfolk Regiment *did* indeed vanish mysteriously at Gallipoli in August 1915, and no satisfactory explanation for their disappearance has ever been found. The question remains – was it *this* battalion of soldiers which the New Zealanders saw walk into the cloud? It seems likely that it must have been. Otherwise, where could their story have come from? And what *did* happen to the missing battalion?

The story of the Royal Norfolk's involvement in the war begins in a small Norfolk town some months earlier. It was here that the regiment, made up of part-time soldiers called Territorials prepared to go off to war. They embarked for Gallipoli on 29 July 1915.

The Gallipoli Peninsula is located in Turkey. Its importance for the Allies lay in the fact that for about 65 kilo-

metres of its length, it is flanked by
a long, narrow channel of water called
the Dardanelles which links the
Mediterranean with the Black Sea. The
Gallipoli campaign was fought for control of this strategic stretch of water
which played an important part in the
plans of Turkey and its German allies.
But the campaign was doomed from
beginning to end. By August, the sear-
ing heat and appalling conditions –
dysentery raged through the camps – had

already claimed the lives of thousands of soldiers. The campaign was extremely slow-moving and the soldiers spent many long days holed up in filthy, crowded trenches, waiting for the action to begin. It was among these chaotic, nightmarish scenes that the First-Fifth battalion of the Royal Norfolk Regiment so mysteriously disappeared.

The battlefield at Gallipoli was a wide, open plain lying between a dried-up salt lake and a ring of high, barren mountains. But many soldiers died before a single shot had been fired, before they had even set foot on the battlefield proper. The trenches were like furnaces and the air was thick with the stench of rotting corpses. Everything, including the meagre food rations, was infested with green flies, nicknamed "corpse flies" because they swarmed over the bodies of dead and injured men. These flies spread dysentery like wildfire through the camp. For the sufferers of this terrible wasting disease, there was no cure or escape. The soldiers who had so far avoided illness were exhausted and morale was at rock bottom. Without any time to get used to the horrors of war, if such as thing is possible, the Norfolks were sent straight to this hellish place to become nothing more than cannon fodder.

The campaign itself was an utter fiasco from beginning to end. The Turkish troops were far better organized than the Allies; they knew the terrain well and they were much better used to the conditions. On the Anzac (Allied) side, confusion and disaster ruled. On the afternoon of 12 August, the Norfolks were sent to clear an area in front of the battlefield of enemy snipers, so that a larger force could advance and attack the Turks the following day. The Norfolks were to receive back-up from the artillery but they were late arriving, and the artillery fire when it came was completely wasted. The advance that afternoon was a crushing failure. The territory was unknown, the strength of the enemy unknown, the commanding officers were uncertain about their objectives and the maps hurriedly issued to them showed another part of the peninsula altogether. As the Norfolks advanced, it soon became clear that attempting to cross the open plain in broad daylight (it was late afternoon by now) had been a big mistake. The First-Fourth Norfolks were forced to the ground by heavy machine-gun fire as they brought up the rear. But the First-Fifth Norfolks, on the right flank, met less opposition and were able to press forward.

The extraordinary events that followed were described by Sir Ian Hamilton, the expedition's Commander-in-Chief, in a report to Lord Kitchener, the Secretary of State for War. This is what the letter said:

"In the course of the fight, creditable in all respects to the [Norfolks], there happened a very mysterious thing. . . Against the yielding forces of the enemy Colonel Sir H. Beauchamp, a bold, self-confident officer, eagerly pressed forward, followed by the best part of the battalion. The fighting grew hotter, and the ground became more wooden and broken. At this stage many men were wounded or grew exhausted with thirst. These found their way back to camp during the night. But the colonel, with 16 officers and 250 men, still kept pushing forward, driving the enemy before him . . . Nothing more was seen or heard of any of them. They charged into the forest and were lost to sight or sound. Not one of them ever came back."

In other words, 267 men had simply vanished into thin air!

At the end of 1915, the Allied forces were evacuated from Gallipoli. The campaign had been an utter fiasco and a humiliating defeat. In the eight short months it had lasted, it had cost the lives of about 46,000 soldiers, a staggering total by any standards. In 1916, a Royal Commission was set up to investigate the defeat. But nothing further was heard of the missing Norfolk battalion until four years later, in 1919, when the British returned to Gallipoli and to ultimate victory. A soldier touring the battlefield found a cap badge belonging to the Royal Norfolk Regiment. He later heard from a Turkish farmer that he had removed a large number of bodies from the area, which turned out to be his land, and thrown them into a nearby ravine. When the bodies were finally recovered on 23 September, the following report was filed:

"We have found the Fifth Norfolk —

there were 180 in all; 122 Norfolk and a few [others]. We could only identify two – Privates Barnaby and Carter. They were scattered over an area of about one square mile (3 sq km), at a distance of at least 800 yards (750 metres) behind the Turkish front line. Many of them had evidently been killed in a farm, as a local Turk, who owns the land, told us that when he came back he found the farm covered with the decomposing bodies of British soldiers which he threw into a small ravine. The whole thing quite bears out the original theory that they did not go very far on, but got mopped up one by one, all except the ones who got into the farmhouse."

But what happened to the other men? Only half of the missing soldiers were accounted for in this report. Their bodies have never been found. Perhaps the New Zealanders were right in their astonishing claim – that they had walked into a cloud and been carried off by alien spacecraft to another world. If not, then what did the New Zealanders actually see? We shall probably never know.

CHAPTER 7
GHOSTS AND HAUNTINGS

GHOSTLY GOINGS-ON

If you have never seen a ghost, and never heard the patter of ghostly footsteps nor ever heard the sound of ghostly voices whispering in your ear, you may be forgiven for thinking that ghosts are most definitely "all in the mind". Of course, some ghostly goings-on can easily be explained away as figments of people's imaginations, especially if they are on their own, at night, and in a spooky place. But so many ghosts and hauntings have been reported over the centuries, that it would be almost impossible to dismiss them *all* as nonsense. Some have been witnessed by children too young to make them up, and by people from all walks of life, from all over the world. Why would they all invent similar experiences? It seems highly unlikely that they could *all* be seeing things.

So, if ghosts *do* exist, what are they and where do they come from? The most common ghostly experiences take place in perfectly ordinary houses, in perfectly normal situations. One theory is that the ghosts that appear in these situations were, in the past, connected to the house in some way, often in a tragic or distressing way. Their very strong emotional ties somehow seem to imprint themselves on the house and come to the fore again when conditions are right. The trigger for this to happen may be the presence in the house of a person who is, wittingly or unwittingly, particularly sensitive or sympathetic to the world of the spirits.

The most famous haunted houses are usually older buildings such as castles, stately homes and churches. But ghosts can, and do, appear anywhere. Almost any building can be haunted, including opera houses, bars, religious shrines, hotels, prisons, even factories. But, despite numerous scientific, and unscientific, ghost-busting investigations, no one has ever managed to solve the mystery of hauntings once and for all. Perhaps they never will. In the meantime, they certainly provide us with plenty of food for thought . . .

Did you know?

One of the most famous haunted buildings is the White House in Washington DC, USA – the official residence of the President of the United States. The most active of the many ghosts which seem to pass in and out of its imposing doors is that of former president, Abraham Lincoln. But he is not alone . . .

THE GHOSTS OF BORLEY RECTORY

Borley Rectory was a gloomy, rambling Victorian building on the banks of the River Stour in Essex, England. It was also, for more than a century, considered to be the most haunted house in England. For over a hundred years, a whole host of ghostly apparitions and incidences were reported in the Rectory. They included sightings of a phantom nun, a headless man and a phantom coach, and showers of stones which appeared from nowhere. There were also poltergeists at work, throwing things about; household objects vanished, then reappeared; writing mysteriously appeared on the Rectory's damp walls. From nearby Borley Church came the eerie sounds of ghostly organ music and monastic chantings, although there were no monks and no one was found playing the organ.

Borley Rectory was built in 1863 on the site of a medieval monastery, so the story went. Soon afterwards, Reverend Henry Dawson Ellis Bull, his wife and their fourteen children moved into the house. They had not been in their new home very long before some very strange things started to happen – they heard footsteps and tapping noises in the middle of the night; bells started ringing and voices whispered up and down the Rectory corridors. One of Reverend Bull's daughters was woken up by someone, or something, slapping her face. Another saw the shadowy figure of an old man, wearing a tall hat, standing by her bedside. A visitor to the Rectory several times saw a ghostly nun wandering the corridors of the house. It was all very unnerving.

From 1892 to 1927, the Rectory passed into the hands of Reverend Bull's son, Harry Bull. During that time, the ghostly apparitions continued as before. A headless man was seen lurking among the bushes outside the house. A phantom coach was seen making its eerie way up the drive. The cook reported that, though she locked the pantry door every night before she went to bed, every morning when she went down to the kitchen it was mysteriously unlocked again although the cook was the only person in the household with the key. On another occasion, several of Harry Bull's sisters caught sight of a young nun who suddenly vanished into thin air.

Then, in 1929, the hauntings took a new turn. Poltergeists, those mischievious, mysterious spirits which move and throw things round, appeared at Borley Rectory for the first time. Strange objects, which did not belong to

any members of the family nor to any of their
visitors, began to be found in various parts of
the house. Among them were pebbles, thrown
from nowhere, keys and medallions, one of
which had the head of St Ignatius engraved on
it.

For five years, from 1930, the Rectory had a
new set of occupants – Reverend Lionel
Algernon Foyster, his wife, Marianne, and his
daughter, Adelaide. Like the Bulls before
them, they soon realized that their new home
was no ordinary house. The haunting continued as frequently as before. A voice was heard
calling out Marianne's name and she was
attacked by an invisible assailant (the first
time anyone had been harmed in Borley
Rectory). More footsteps were heard in the
dead of night, pattering ceaselessly up and
down the corridors. Strange smells wafted
about the house – the scent of lavender was
particularly strong. Mysterious scraps of
paper appeared, and messages continued to be
scrawled on the walls. Many of these were too
scribbled to be legible but one message seemed
to spell out the words:

**"Marianne, Get Help. To die
unrepentant bothers me."**

Visitors to the Rectory were also subjected to bizarre, ghostly ordeals. In 1931, a man called Edwin Whitehouse, who later became a Benedictine monk, was visiting the Rectory with his uncle and aunt. During his stay, a fire suddenly started in a room which was no longer used. As Edwin rushed to put out the flames, a pebble the size of an egg, fell out of the fire. Reverend Foyster decided to conduct an exorcism in the hope of ridding the house of its spooks once and for all. As the service progressed, Edwin and his aunt were pelted by falling stones which suddenly appeared out of thin air.

By now, the mysterious happenings in Borley Rectory had aroused the interest of ghost-hunters, newspaper reporters, scientists and the public in general. In 1937, a man called Harry Price, who founded Britain's National Laboratory of Psychical Research decided to rent the Rectory for a year, to give himself time for a thorough investigation of its invisible visitors. He placed an advert in the Times newspaper, asking for people "of leisure and intelligence, intrepid, critical, and unbiased" to join a team of observers. More than two hundred people applied for the job. Of these, he chose the forty most suitable.

Some of the team heard unexplained voices

and other noises. Others saw objects move through the air. One man was hit by a bar of soap which suddenly sailed through the air towards him. Another member of the team, a well-known and well-respected philosopher, reported that a thermometer had suddenly dropped by ten degrees for no apparent reason.

Unfortunately, Harry Price and his research methods were so dubious that the whole mystery of Borley Rectory was almost dismissed as a carefully-planned hoax. Price claimed to have seen some two hundred different ghosts at the Rectory which he publicized through a series of lectures, books and broadcasts. Critics claimed that he had exploited the house for his own short glimpse of fame and fortune. Price died in 1948, but in 1956, his method of investigation was severely criticized by the Society of Psychical Research which carried out its own independent investigation of the Rectory. They suggested that Price had misrepresented many of the so-called hauntings and had produce some of the strange phenomena himself! In 1969, another examination of the evidence seemed to clear Price's name and many people sprang to his defence. The damage to his reputation, and that of Borley Rectory, had, however, been done.

In 1939, the Rectory was burned to the ground in a mysterious blaze. On the night of the fire, two dark figures were seen leaving the building, though the only person known to have been in it at the time was its new owner, Captain Gregson. Several onlookers claimed to have seen the face of a young girl peering out of an upstairs window. All that remained of the original Borley site was the coach house and the parish church, opposite the house.

But the fire did not put an end to the ghostly phenomena. They continued as before. One man heard the thunder of hooves pass close by to him as he walked by the Rectory. When he looked round, there was no sign of a horse nor of a carriage. During the war, mysterious lights were seen shining from the windows, although no one was living in the house at the time.

In 1943, the whole site was dug up and a row of council houses built on the former rectory garden. During the excavations, fragments of a woman's skull were found in the ground, together with several pendants engraved with religious symbols.

So, what was it about Borley Rectory that marked it out for such a haunting? Legend says that the Rectory was built on the site of a thirteenth-century monastery which was linked to a convent a few kilometres away at a place called Bures. A monk fell in love with one of the nuns but the couple were caught as they tried to elope, and killed. Phantoms of the nun, the coach in which she tried to escape and a headless driver were frequently seen at the Rectory.

Another story tells how, in the seventeenth century, a young French nun, called Marie Lairre, was forced to leave her convent at Le Havre to marry a member of the wealthy Waldegrave family who lived in Borley. The

story tells how, on the night of 17 May 1667, Marie was strangled by her fiancé, in a building which stood on the site of the rectory. Her body was buried in the cellar. Was it her ghost which roamed the corridors of the Rectory for all those long, lonely years?

THE GHOST OF MARY TUDOR

Many historic buildings, such as castles and stately homes, claim to be haunted, often by the ghosts of the present owners' long-dead ancestors or by their famous guests. Sawston Hall, near Cambridge, England, is no exception. It can boast a very famous ghost indeed.

The hall was built in Tudor times, on the site of an ancient Roman settlement. For 450 years, it was the ancestral home of the Huddlestons, a Roman Catholic family who suffered for their beliefs in the religious confusion and bigotry following the death of King Henry VIII.

In 1553, a very special visitor arrived at Sawston Hall. Her name was Mary Tudor and she was Henry VIII's elder daughter. She spent the night in the Tapestry Room at Sawston Hall. (Today, the bed she is said to have slept in now occupies pride of place among the hall's many historical exhibits.) That night, her brother, King Edward VI died, leaving the way open for his sister Mary to be crowned queen.

Before this could happen, though, in fact before news of Edward's death even reached Mary, the Duke of Northumberland, a powerful and scheming man hatched a plot to keep Mary from the throne. He captured the Tower of London, and proclaimed his daughter-in-law, Lady Jane Grey, queen. Then he sent a message to Mary, requesting that she return to London at once to visit her sick brother. Once she was back in London, Northumberland intended to take her prisoner. Meanwhile, back at Sawston Hall, Mary slept peacefully in her bed, oblivious to the scheming going on around her.

At the crack of dawn on 8 July 1553, she was hurriedly awoken by John Huddleston, the owner of the hall. Somehow he had learned of the danger she faced if she returned to London. He smuggled her out of the hall, disguised as a humble milkmaid. As it turns out, Mary escaped in the nick of time. Having ridden a safe distance from the house, she and the few companions who had escaped with her turned and glanced back at it. The hall was in flames, set alight by Northumberland's men when they failed to find Mary as expected. Mary is said to have been deeply moved at the sight of her friend's misfortunes.

"Let it burn," she said to her companions. Her next words were prophetic:

"When I am queen I will build Master Huddleston a finer house."

And she kept her word. In 1585, a new version of Sawston Hall was constructed from stones taken from Cambridge Castle. It still stands today and is still and is still occupied by members of the Huddleston family.

Mary died on 17 November 1558, having reigned as queen for just five years. Since then, her ghost has been seen many times at Sawston Hall, strolling regally through the garden and grounds. The Tapestry Room, where she spent that fateful night, survived the fire which destroyed the rest of the hall. From it, the haunting sounds of a spinet being played could often be heard, although no such instrument had ever been kept in the room.

Was the spinet player Mary's ghost, or the ghost of one of her ladies-in-waiting? The sound of girlish laughter has also been heard coming from that room. But who it comes from, no one knows.

THE ANGELS OF MONS

The Battle of Mons, one of the hardest and most bitterly fought of the First World War, took place on 26 August 1914. A month later, a sensational report of the battle appeared in the *London Evening News*. It began a controversy which has lasted ever since.

The author of the report was a Welsh journalist, Arthur Machen. He wrote of how the tiny British Expeditionary Force (BEF), heavily outnumbered by the enemy by three to one, were saved by the sudden and mysterious appearance of a ghostly platoon of angels. By positioning themselves between the BEF and the enemy, the angels caused the enemy soldiers to retreat in terror and confusion.

When the article appeared in the newspaper, most of the survivors of the battle were still with their regiments in France. They had not yet returned and could not back up, nor deny, the extraordinary story being circulated at home. The following summer, however, another report, published anonymously in a parish magazine in Bristol, claimed to be the true statement of a British officer who had witnessed the whole amazing incident. In the statement, the officer told how, at Mons, his company had been forced into retreat by a unit of the German cavalry. They tried to reach a place where they could stand and fight, but the Germans got there first. As the British soldiers prepared to meet almost certain death, the most amazing thing happened – before their disbelieving eyes, a troop of angels descended from heaven and took up a position between the British and German soldiers. The German horses were terrified and bolted.

Various other accounts, supposedly gleaned from eyewitnesses, followed this one. Another report told how, on another occasion, a battalion had been saved from near certain disaster by the arrival of a squadron of phantom cavalry.

Over the years, however, doubts began to creep into the minds of those investigating the reports. None of the accounts of the mysterious ghostly angels were first hand. They came from officers who wished to remain anonymous for fear of being labelled as cranks and damaging their promotion prospects. Years later, even Arthur Machen himself, the journalist of the original newspaper report, is said to have admitted that he made the whole thing up!

But the mystery did not disappear completely. There were too many reports from returning soldiers of strange events taking place at Mons, for them all to be dismissed. It became clear that something out of the ordinary had taken place but whether a battalion of ghostly angels had in fact saved the British Army, no one knew.

THE MYSTERIOUS MOVING COFFINS

In August 1812, the massive, rock-cut family tomb of the Chase family at Christ Church on the Caribbean island of Barbados was opened to receive the body of the slave-owner and head of the family, Thomas Chase. As the huge, marble door which sealed the tomb was moved aside and the coffin carried down the dank, stone steps into the gloomy vault, it became clear that something out of the ordinary had happened. The tomb already contained three coffins. Two of these belonged to two daughters from the Chase family – one who had died in 1808, and the other early in 1812. The third coffin belonged to Mrs Thomasina Goddard, who had died in 1807, and who was a member of the Walrond family, a family of rich planters who built the original tomb in the eighteenth century. It was later bought from them by Thomas Chase.

As the eyes of the mourners and coffin-carriers gradually became used to the dim light inside the tomb, a very strange sight greeted them. One of the three coffins was lying on its side. The two others had been stood on their ends, upside down, in the one corner. It was obvious that the tomb had been violated. But there was no sign of a break-in. The coffins were put back in their original places and the door to the tomb was resealed. But the rumours had already started. Thomas Chase had been known as a cruel and ruthless man – there was even a story that his daughter, Dorcas, who died a month before her father had starved herself to death because of his vicious nature. In all probability, people said, the tomb had been desecrated by former slaves or other people who Chase had treated badly. But no one knew for sure.

Four years later, in September 1816, the tomb was opened again for a tiny coffin containing the body of eleven-month-old Samuel Brewster Ames, another member of the Chase family. And once again, the vault was found in a state of extreme disorder. All four of the coffins it contained had been thrown across the floor. The immensely heavy, lead-plated coffin belonging to Thomas Chase himself, which had taken eight men to carry to its final resting place, was found leaning against the wall. Again, the coffins were carefully put back into their original places and the tomb was resealed.

By the time of the next family funeral, just eight weeks later, the story of the strange tomb and its moving coffins had spread around the island, and a huge crowd turned up for the burial ceremony. They were not to be disappointed. Yet again, despite the fact that the tomb door had been resealed even more securely than ever and the cement seal showed no sign of being tampered with, the coffins inside were in a state of great disarray, tumbled about across the floor. While people still believed that the violation of the tomb was an act of revenge, they could not explain how the vandals had got inside. The mystery was growing deeper with each new burial.

The wooden coffin belonging to Mrs Goddard had, by now, almost disintegrated, perhaps because of being so roughly handled. It was tied back together with pieces of wire and placed against one wall. To create more space – the vault was getting rather crowded by this time – the smaller, children's coffins were stacked on top of the coffins belonging to the adult. Then the great marble door was once more cemented back into place, and the vault resealed.

The fame of the moving coffins spread quickly and crowds of curious sight-seers flocked to the Christ Church to see the tomb for themselves, much to the displeasure of the church's rector, Reverend Thomas Orderson. Try as he might to keep the good temper which his role required, he found his patience sorely tried. Time and again, he explained that he and a magistrate had made a careful and thorough search of the tomb the last time it was opened. But they had found no sign of anyone having broken into the tomb – there was no secret door leading into it, and no holes had been hacked through the solid rock walls or ceiling. Neither did he think that the mystery could be put down to flooding. The tomb was made of solid limestone and, though it lay a metre below ground level, it was highly unlikely to have flooded. Besides, there was no sign of any water damage either. Reverend Orderson also dismissed as nonsense some of the more outlandish theories which were being proposed, blaming ghostly activity or a curse for the shifting positions of the coffins. So who or what was responsible? After all, the coffins could not possibly have moved by themselves . . .

In July 1819, the tomb was opened for the next and final time. This time, the occasion was the burial of Mrs Thomasina Clarke who was buried in a coffin made of cedar wood. By now, the coffins had attracted world-wide interest and the burial was an internationally attended event. The cement around the marble door took some time to chip away – the door had been sealed and resealed many times by now – and even then, it still refused to budge. After a great deal of pushing and shoving, the door did finally open, only to reveal the reason why it had seemed to be stuck – Thomas Chase's heavy coffin had been dragged across the floor and jammed up against it! And, as on every previous occasion, every one of the other coffins had been moved too. The vandals had been at it again.

It was then that the Governor of Barbados, Lord Combermere, stepped in. He had been one of the first people to go inside the tomb and had witnessed first-hand the bizarre movement of the coffins. He now ordered a thorough search of the tomb. But the search only reinforced what Reverend Orderson had already discovered – that there was no secret trapdoor. In fact, there was no way whatsoever by which vandals could have forced their way into the tomb. Neither was there any sign of floodwater having seeped in. Lord Combermere ordered the coffins to be restacked again, in an orderly way, and had the marble door resealed. Before the final seal was put in place, however, the Governor laid his trap. He ordered the floor of the tomb to be sprinkled with sand, so that any footprints left by the intruders could be clearly seen. Then the door was cemented shut, and sealed with Lord Combermere's private family seal.

The following year, after local people had reported hearing noises coming from the tomb, Lord Combermere decided to launch another investigation, and to find out whether his precautions had worked. Nine men, the Governor among them, set off to visit the tomb. They found that the seals around the door were intact and that no one had touched the new cement. But when they eventually opened the door, they could not believe their eyes. Once again, the tomb was in turmoil and each of the coffins had been moved from its place. A child's coffin lay higgledy-piggledy on the steps which led down into the burial vault; Thomas Chase's enormous coffin lay upside down on the floor. The only coffin which still lay peacefully where they had left it last time was the little, crumbling wooden coffin belonging to Mrs Goddard.

Stranger still was the fact that the sand which Lord Combermere had had sprinkled over the floor, showed no traces of footprints or other marks whatsoever . . .

Lord Combermere and his colleagues were forced to admit defeat. Yet again, they had hunted high and low for a secret entrance into the tomb. Yet again, they had found nothing. The mystery was no closer to being solved that it had been at the time of Thomas Chase's burial. The Governor gave orders for the coffins to be removed and to be buried in another tomb, on another part of the island. The Christ Church tomb remains empty to this day.

Since that time, more than one hundred and fifty years ago, no one has been able to come up with a satisfactory explanation for the mysterious moving coffins. The two natural explanations, that the coffins were tumbled about by floodwaters entering the tomb or by slight earth tremors, raise more questions than they answer. For example, surely any flooding would have affected the sand on the tomb floor? And surely the rector of the church would have noticed if it rained hard enough to flood the graveyard? If the coffins had been moved by earth tremors, surely these would have been strong enough to disturb some of the nearby tombs too? None showed any sign of disturbance.

Sir Arthur Conan Doyle, the creator of the detective, Sherlock Holmes, suggested that supernatural forces had been at work inside the Christ Church tomb. He thought that these forces may have objected to the lead used to line the coffins because it stopped the bodies inside from decaying quickly. He further suggested that these forces may have been made stronger and more violent by the fact that Thomas Chase and one of his daughters had committed suicide, at that time classed as unholy. Local people firmly believed that some kind of voodoo was at work in the tomb, as revenge for Thomas Chase's ill treatment of his slaves. And finally, several theories suggest that the coffins were moved about by poltergeists. The real cause remains a mystery . . .

THE FLYING DUTCHMAN
Ghost Ship of the High Seas

Legend has it that any ship or sailor which sights the phantom *Flying Dutchman* is bound to meet with bad luck. But what was this strange ghost-ship and how did it get its unlucky reputation? For more than three hundred years, the story of the *Flying Dutchman* trying to sail round the Cape of Good Hope against strong winds, and never succeeding, had been the most famous ghost story of the sea. The ship is said to sail back and forth on its endless voyage, with no hope of ever reaching its destination, while its ancient crew cry out to passing ships for help as they endlessly raise and lower her sails. Many literary and musical works have been inspired by the story, and many superstitions have arisen from it. One says that any sailor who see the *Flying Dutchman* will die soon afterwards – many are said to have met this unfortunate end. Another old tale tells how the ship always vanishes into a storm as soon as another ship gets close enough to it to call to its crew. No one knows whether the real *Flying Dutchman* ever existed but this is the story often told about the ghostly vessel.

Old records show that in 1680, a Dutch sailing

ship, captained by Hendrik Van der Decken, set sail from Amsterdam bound for the Dutch settlement of Batavia in the East Indies. Captain Van der Decken was a brave and adventurous sailor. He was also famous for having no scruples whatsoever – his reputation often went before him. He was, however, a competent, skilful sailor and the ship's owners had no hesitation in entrusting the command of their precious ship into his capable hands. Perhaps they hadn't heard him when he had been boasting in the harbour tavern about returning from the voyage as a wealthy man?

The voyage began well enough. As Van der Decken and his crew sailed south into tropical seas, the weather remained clear, sunny and set fair. Near the Cape of Good Hope, however, the scene began to change. A tropical gale suddenly blew up out of nowhere and began to rip into the ship, tearing its sails into shreds and destroying its rudder. And the storm showed no signs of abating. As the days dragged into weeks, the ship was tossed to and fro by gigantic waves off the Cape, completely unable to make any headway against the terrifying force of the south-easterly gale which blew night and day. Captain Van der Decken was furious. He tried every trick of navigation he knew to try to bring the ship to order – after all, he had boasted to the crew that no storm had ever made him turn back yet. But no matter how hard he tried or how hard he cursed, he failed to bring the vessel around the Cape.

The crew begged the captain to turn back – the ship could not survive such a beating for much longer.

"If we keep trying to round the Cape in this wind," they pleaded, "we shall sink."

Captain Van der Decken took no notice. In fact, the more they begged him to turn back, the more stubborn he became. When a group of men tried to force him to listen to them, he simply picked up their ring-leader and threw him overboard.

Meanwhile, the storm raged all around and still the captain could not get the ship to sail on.

Legend says that the Devil, taking advantage of Captain Van der Decken's malicious frame of mind, decided to intervene and make the captain an offer he could not, in the circumstances, possibly refuse. One night, he appeared to the captain in a dream and suggested that he should fight against God's attempts to stop him sailing round the Cape. Captain Van der Decken took very little persuasion. He agreed to listen to the Devil and to defy God.

But retribution was swift. An angel appeared and commanded that Captain Van der Decken be punished for his wickedness. His fate was to roam the seas forever, with no hope of ever reaching land. The ship itself would eventually run aground, and the crew grow old and die, but Van der Decken must keep an endless watch until Doomsday.

The ship never reached its destination in Batavia. It is said to have roamed the seas ever since, spelling doom to any sailor unlucky enough to catch sight of it. Many people claim that they have, indeed, seen the *Flying Dutchman*, sailing its lonely course. On a baking hot day in March 1939, a group of holiday-makers were relaxing beside the warm waters of the Indian Ocean at the tip of South Africa. Suddenly, a mighty sailing ship, fully rigged, sailed out of the heat haze hanging over the sea. The last time a ship of this type had been seen in these waters had been more than two hundred years before. The sunbathers were stunned and excited as they watched the ship. What

could it be? And where had it come from? The
following report appeared later in the press:

*"With uncanny volition the ship sailed
steadily on as the Glencairn beachfold, shaken
from their lethargy, stood about keenly dis-
cussing the whys and wherefores of the vessel
which seemed to be bent on self-destruction
somewhere on the sands of Strandfontein. Just
as the excitement reached its climax, however,
the mystery ship vanished into thin air as
strangely as it had come."*

In the days following the appearance of the
ghostly ship, many theories were put forward
about its true identity. Scientists insisted that
the watchers had seen a mirage and that the
ship was actually a distorted reflection of
another, real ship several hundred kilometres
away. But, according to several of the eyewitnesses, the ship was unlike any modern vessel
that might be sailing the seas. It was, without
a doubt, a merchant sailing ship, of a type
which was built and sailed in the seventeenth
century. Another eyewitness even went so far
as to identify the name of the ship.

"Let the sceptics say what they will," she
announced. "That ship was none other than
the *Flying Dutchman*."

The last recorded sighting of the *Flying*

Dutchman was in September 1942. Four people sitting out on their balcony, in Cape Town, South Africa, suddenly saw the ghostly ship sail into the bay, then disappear from sight again.

Did you know?

In World War II, the crew of an American warship, the *USS Kennison*, twice reported seeing "ghost ships" in the middle of the ocean. The ships appeared, then disappeared in front of their eyes.

THINGS THAT GO BUMP IN THE NIGHT . . .

The word "poltergeist" means "noisy spirit", and noisy these ghostly presences certainly are, though whether they are in fact spirits remains open to question. They are the ghosts which make things go "bump in the night". Their reputed powers include sending objects flying across rooms, opening and closing doors, tapping on the walls, making noises after dark and causing crockery and pottery to smash. This, say some investigators, is the poltergeists' way of trying to communicate with living human beings. But what their message is, no one seems to know. Whatever poltergeists are, and whatever their intention, they remain one of the most baffling and mysterious of phenomena. If they are ghosts or spirits, then their chief characteristic seems to be mischief making. Could this be why they usually seem to operate when children or young people are present? Read on . . .

· Poltergeists from the past

One of the earliest known cases of poltergeist activity dates back as far as AD 858. It was recorded in an ancient German chronicle, called the *Annales Fuldenses*. The incident took place in a farmhouse at Bingen, a picturesque town on the banks of the River Rhine. The writer of the chronicles describes how an "evil spirit" threw stones at the farmhouse and made the walls shudder and shake as if someone was hitting them with a large hammer. The "evil spirit" also set fire to the farmer's crops which had just been harvested and brought in. It also accused him of being wicked, corrupt and sinful. An exorcist was sent by the Bishop of Mainz but he apparently failed to have any impact on the poltergeist at all.

· The Cock Lane ghost

One of the most famous poltergeist cases of all time was that of the Cock Lane "ghost" of 1759. It became so famous that many of the great names of the time – Samuel Johnson and Horace Walpole among them – were anxious to play a part in the investigations.

The story began in Cock Lane, London, at the home of a clerk, called Richard Parsons. Parsons had recently taken in two lodgers – a retired innkeeper, William Kent and his common-law wife, Fanny Lynes. Kent had in fact been married to Fanny's sister, Elizabeth, who had died in childbirth. The couple fell in love but the law prevented them from getting married because of their previous relationship to each other. Not long after the couple had moved into the Parsons' house, Kent had to go away from home for a few nights. Fanny was pregnant and afraid. She asked the Parsons' eldest daughter, ten-year old Elizabeth, to sleep with her to keep her company while Kent was away.

There was not much sleep to be had that night, however, nor for the several nights that followed. Fanny and Elizabeth were kept awake for hours by loud noises – knocking and scraping noises coming up through the floor. At first, they thought it must be the shoemaker who lived next door working on late into the night. But the shoemaker said he had been fast asleep by that time. The only other explanation seemed to be that the house was infested by a "rattling ghost". But what on earth was to be done about it?

Soon afterwards, Fanny Lynes died of smallpox. William Kent moved out of the Parsons' house, and, two years' later, had married someone else. But the knockings still continued. A priest was called in to try to exorcise the "ghost". He was able to communicate with the spirit by knocking, using a code of one knock for yes and two for no. In this way, he discovered the identity of the spirit – it was none other than Fanny Lynes herself who claimed that she had been poisoned by William Kent and now wanted to see justice done.

It suited Richard Parsons very well to hear Kent accused of being a murderer. He had borrowed some money from his lodger and failed to keep up the repayments. Kent was now threatening to take him to court if he did not pay back the sum in full, and at once. And so, he did not let on that the knocking noises had begun *before* Fanny Lynes' death . . . Instead, he spread the news of Kent's guilt all over London. When Kent heard what he was being accused of, he came to Cock Lane to hear the evidence for himself. He was furious and dismissed the whole thing as nonsense. By now, the case was famous. Other investigators also came to hear the ghost. For them, however, it remained ominously silent.

Finally, William Kent had had enough. He decided to prosecute Richard Parsons for libel. It was up to Parsons to prove that he and his family were innocent of any charges. Elizabeth Parsons was told that, if the ghost did not show itself this time, her father and mother would be sent to prison. The young girl was, quite naturally, terrified by the thought of losing both her parents, and decided to do something about it. Unfortunately, she was spotted by some servants making knocking noises on a wooden board. The court denounced the ghost as fake, caused deliberately by the Parsons. They sentenced Parsons himself to two years in prison, and three sessions standing in the pillories. Mrs Parsons was sent to prison for a year; another woman who claimed to have talked to the ghost received six months. Even the priest who had come to do the exorcism was given a huge fine.

But many of the people present in the courtroom felt that the Parsons had been very hard done by. A collection was even made to help them. Many witnesses claimed that it would have been impossible for Elizabeth to have faked the initial knocking noises, and that a genuine poltergeist could be the only culprit. After all, Elizabeth was exactly the right age to be the focus of poltergeist activity.

• The Great Amherst Mystery

This remarkable case happened in Amherst, Nova Scotia, in 1878. It was later recorded in a book called *The Great Amherst Mystery* by a stage magician, Walter Hubbell, who had been invited into the house of the Teed family to investigate several incidences of poltergeist activity, involving an 18-year-old girl, Esther Cox. She lived in the house with her brother-in-law, Daniel Teed, the house's owner, her two sisters (one of whom was married to Daniel), her brother and Daniel's brother and his two sons. The house was always crowded and always noisy.

The poltergeist disturbances began the year before when Esther's boyfriend, Bob MacNeal, had threatened her with a gun. Luckily, someone came by and disturbed him. MacNeal fled Amherst in shame and never returned. Over the following weeks and months, the Teed household was tormented by poltergeist activities, all of which seemed to be centred on Esther. She and her sister Jane were kept awake at night by strange, mouse-like rustling and scratching noises. A cardboard box leapt straight into the air. Esther herself suffered a great deal of physical punishment. Her body swelled up like a balloon, then returned to normal after a loud banging noise was heard. She was stabbed with a pen and a fork, and hit over the head with a broom. Her pillows and bedclothes were flung from the bed. She complained that she kept getting tingling feelings, like short, sharp electric shocks, running through her body. Small fires broke out and furniture shifted around the house. Perhaps most frightening of all was the writing that appeared spontaneously on the wall above her bed, in front of several witnesses. It read:

"Esther, you are mine to kill."

Walter Hubbell, magician and psychic investigator, meanwhile, was running his own tests to prove that poltergeists were at work. He succeeded in "communicating" with the rattling ghosts, and he proclaimed that they were indeed genuine because they could tell the date of the coins inside his pocket without seeing them. Esther herself blamed the phenomena on spirits who "spoke to her". She even had a name for the most troublesome spirit – she called him Bob Nickle, a name remarkably like that of her violent ex-boyfriend. The doctors who examined her said that she was undoubtedly mentally disturbed, but they had no explanation for the string of bizarre experiences she had undergone. And, when a nearby barn burned down, Esther was accused of arson and sentenced to four months in prison. And the poltergeist activity suddenly and mysteriously stopped.

· Setting a trap for a poltergeist

Herr Adam, a respected lawyer practising in Bavaria, southern Germany, attempted to outwit the poltergeists who began to disrupt his life. The events began in November 1967 – light bulbs in his office began to shatter without warning; lampshades fell off; telephones started to ring for no reason. Herr Adam had had no previous experience of supernatural happenings, and was not the sort of person to make them up. He was baffled by what was happening. He decided to call in some technical experts to check the electricity supply to his office – perhaps the events could be simply explained by an electrical fault? Their findings were even more mysterious. At times, as they monitored the electricity supply, there were such enormous surges in power that the recording device's needles tore through the graph paper underneath. But never once did it cause any of the fuses to blow, as might have been expected.

Next, Herr Adam took his case to Hans Bender, a professor of parapsychology, who specialized in spirits and poltergeists. He set a series of traps to see if there was a hoaxer at work. All these tests proved to be negative.

Professor Bender interviewed several people who had witnessed the events, and came to the conclusion that this was indeed the work of poltergeists who were focusing their attention not on Herr Adam himself, but on his 19-year-old clerk, Anne-Marie. For it turned out that the bizarre events had started at exactly the time Anne-Marie had begun work in Herr Adam's office – there had been no such problems before her arrival. More tellingly, the events stopped when she went on leave and began again when she returned to work. When she left the office altogether and started another job somewhere else, the incidents stopped altogether. It was reported, however, that strange things did begin to happen at her new employers.

Anne-Marie was tested by psychologists and doctors, but they could find nothing at all wrong with her.

· Popping corks

Another amazing poltergeist case began in the bedroom of a house on Long Island, near New York, USA. The house belonged to James Herrmann. Mr Herrmann had two children – Lucille, aged 13, and James, aged 12.

One day, the top of a bottle of holy water suddenly unscrewed itself and the contents of the bottle poured on to the bedroom floor. In the bathroom, a bottle of shampoo also opened in the same mysterious way, as did a bottle of medicine. Meanwhile, other bottles in the kitchen and cellar began opening, one after the other. No one had touched them.

Then, as Mr Herrmann was cleaning his teeth, he watched in amazement as a bottle of medicine flew across the room and smashed into the wall. Again, no one had touched it or moved it in any way.

The police were called to the Herrmann house to investigate. The officer on duty, James Hughes, listened politely to their story but privately thought they must be making the whole thing up. Until, that is, he witnessed the events they described first hand. As he sat talking to the family in their living room, more bottles began to pop open by themselves. Hughes could not believed his eyes. Another officer, Joseph Tozzi, later joined the case. Like Hughes, he was at a loss to explain what he saw, despite the fact that he did not believe in any way in the supernatural. Tozzi not only witnessed the opening bottles; he also watched a china figurine fly across the dining room and smash into a desk.

By now, the Herrmanns had had enough. The whole family went to stay with relatives for a while. But on the very first night of their return, however, a glass bowl leapt into the air, landed on the floor and smashed into pieces . . .

So, what are these mysterious poltergeists? Some people dismiss so-called poltergeist activity as a case of mind over matter where people can make objects move by an immense effort of will. Others are convinced that the poltergeists are fakes – and that the children involved are often themselves the culprits. This has certainly proved to be the case on several occasions. Other people believe that poltergeists are "earth-bound" spirits – the spirits of dead people who for some reason are doomed to roam the earth forever. They remain linked with one particular place and can only show themselves if they lock into a human being's own energy supply. This human being is often a child or a teenager.

Whatever the truth of the matter, there have been thousands of cases of poltergeist activity reported from all over the world. Hundreds more are reported each year, most of which are easy to witness and investigate. No purely scientific explanation had ever been offered which fully solves the mystery of poltergeists. But don't have nightmares. Any bumps in the night which you might hear are probably caused by the cat!

CHAPTER 8

MYSTERY NEWS

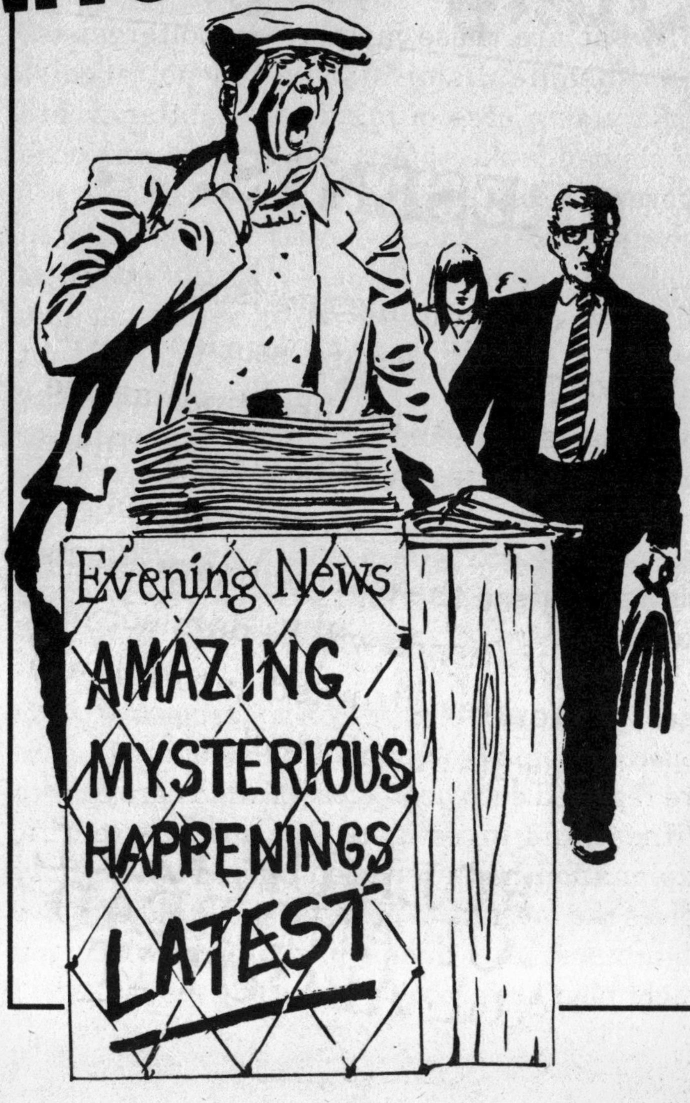

The Daily Mystery

PRESENTS. . .

. . . yet more mesmerising, mind-boggling, mystery stories which have all hit the headlines at one time or other. Slip some of these into any ordinary conversation and see the extraordinary effects. Your friends will be dazzled; your enemies stunned into silence. Results guaranteed!

ROLL UP, ROLL UP AND READ ALL ABOUT IT . . .

Up, up and away...

On 1 December 1881, Walter Powell, MP, went for a balloon trip with two of his friends. Perfectly harmless, you might think. Indeed, so far so good. The balloon came down to land on a beach in Dorset, southern England and the two friends got out. Walter Powell picked up his coat and was all set to follow. But just as he started to climb out of the basket, the balloon gave a violent jerk and rose high up into the clouds again, with Powell still on board. He was gone, never to be seen again.

A search was quickly launched and, for the next three days, the beaches were combed and the sea surveyed – it seemed most likely that he had crashed in the English Channel. The search was spectacularly unsuccessful – neither the balloon nor its passenger were anywhere to be found.

Various theories were put forward. Immediately after Powell's disappearance, reports poured in of mysterious bright lights being seen in the sky on both sides of the Channel. Two days later, an unidentified glowing object was spotted in the skies over Cherbourg, France. Two weeks later, a ship's captain sighted another glowing object in the sky over eastern Scotland. It was like the "gondola of a balloon", he said, "which seemed alternately to increase and diminish in size". Next day, a similar object was seen off the Spanish coast.

Were these mysterious objects linked to each other? Were they, indeed, linked to William Powell's balloon? We shall never know . . .

The vanishing army

It's December 1937. Japan and China have been at war for six long months. The Chinese are being pushed back. Shanghai falls and Japanese troops advance on the city of Nanking.

In a last-ditch effort to avert disaster, the Chinese commander, Colonel Li Fu Sien, sent an urgent request for three thousand more soldiers to reinforce his exhausted troops. He positioned them along the Yangtze River, close to a strategically important bridge. They were heavily armed and well prepared. While they waited for the expected Japanese assault, the colonel returned to his headquarters. Early in the morning, he was woken from his sleep by an aide bringing an extraordinary message — contact with the army had completely broken down! What had happened to them? Was their equipment faulty? Had the Japanese launched a suprise attack under cover of night? The colonel acted at once and drove down to investigate. He couldn't believe what he saw — the guns were still in position, but of the men, there was not a sign. They seemed to have vanished into thin air.

The colonel did find a small group of about a hundred soldiers still in place near the bridge. But they were as astonished by the news as he was. If the soldiers had surrendered to the Japanese, even if they had deserted en masse, the noise and commotion would surely have alerted the others to the danger. But the soldiers had seen and heard nothing. Neither had they seen anyone cross or pass close by the bridge during the night.

There was no chance of the mystery being solved in the turmoil of the days that followed. The Japanese army crossed the river and within two days, Nanking had fallen. The city was torn apart by one of the most appalling and most ruthless massacres in history, so cruel that many soldiers were recalled to Japan to answer for their terrible actions. No one gave the missing troops another thought — that would have to wait for more peaceful times.

In fact, the mystery of the missing soldiers was never properly investigated and was certainly never solved. A token effort was made to consult the Japanese military reports but these made no mention of the men, nor of three thousand prisoners of war arriving in any Japanese camps. Perhaps, compared to the horrors of the war raging around them, these things just didn't seem that important.

Travels through time?

On an October morning in 1593, a strange-looking man stood in the square in front of the royal palace in Mexico City. The square was full, as usual, of people going about their daily business, and of soldiers. But this particular soldier stood out from the rest. He was wearing a different uniform, one not seen in the city before, and carried a gun of unknown type.

The soldier was brought to the attention of the local authorities who questioned him closely. Who was he and where had he come from? Which army did he belong to? What was he doing in the square? The soldier replied that he'd been given orders, earlier that morning, to guard the governor's palace in Manila where he was stationed. The governor had been killed the night before and there were fears for the rest of his family.

But Manila was thousands of miles away in the Philippines. When he was told that he was in Mexico, the soldier seemed completely baffled. "I knew it couldn't be Manila," he said. "But I saw the palace and thought I'd get my bearings there. But how I got here, I have no idea whatsoever!"

"A likely story," the authorities muttered, and locked the soldier away in the city jail. But two months later, their astonishment grew when a ship arrived from the Philippines. It brought news that the governor had indeed been murdered, and on the very night the soldier had said. They were able to identify his uniform as that of a palace guard and to vouch for him in general. All along, he'd been telling the truth. He was quickly released and sent back to Manila. But how he arrived in Mexico, out of the blue, remains a mystery to this day.

The conjuror vanishes

Is it possible for a human being to vanish into thin air. No? Yet there are many reports to the

contrary, including the mysterious disappearance of the Chinese soldiers above. No one
knows how it happens. The cynics say that
there must be a perfectly logical explanation.
Perhaps the whole thing has been purposely
stage-managed to make it appear like magic.
But, so far, none of these perfectly logical
explanations have been able to explain very
much at all. Take, for example, the case of the
vanishing conjuror.

It was a Thursday afternoon in New York.
At the Paramount Theatre, the matinee was
about to begin. The star of the show, the conjuror, William Kneff, stepped out from behind
the lush velvet curtain and began his patter,
just as he had many, many times before. Then,
a most extraordinary thing began to happen.
As the audience watched in amazement,
William Kneff began to fade. His body became
more and more transparent until, before their
eyes, he utterly and completely disappeared.
His voice, however, continued its patter, clear
and normal as before. It was very weird!

Things became weirder still, a few minutes
later. Kneff gradually began to reappear and
was soon standing on stage again, looking
completely unperturbed by his experience. The
audience burst into rapturous applause,
assuming that this was simply (if brilliantly)

part of the routine. When the show was over, someone asked Kneff how he'd done it. He seemed surprised by the question – he was aware that he had vanished and had no idea how it could have happened. He did admit, however, that the same thing had happened during a show some three years earlier. Stranger still was the occasion only a few nights before, when he'd been sitting at home watching television. Suddenly, his wife had screamed. Keff had reached out a comforting arm to touch her but she'd only screamed louder and jumped out of the way. Keff left the room to fetch a glass of water for her. When he returned, she rushed towards him, sobbing. It turned out, that for a few minutes, she had not been able to see him – once again, he had vanished into thin air.

No satisfactory explanation has ever been put forward.

Unidentified flying hay?

On a warm afternoon in July, at the end of the last century, some farm workers near the Welsh town of Wrexham were astonished to see several large clumps of hay flying through the sky above their heads. More puzzling still, it seemed to be flying under its own steam!

The flying hay headed north, against the wind and only began to disintegrate some five miles later, when it sailed over Wrexham town itself. A local newspaper wrote that "it caused much consternation while passing over the town".

Were there strange forces at work on that balmy summer's day? A mischievious poltergeist perhaps? Or was it an elaborate, and ingenious, practical joke?

OFF COURSE —
ships that sailed themselves

The most famous example of a ship that sailed itself is, of course, the *Mary Celeste* (see page 95). But she's not alone! There are a great many cases of ships being suddenly and inexplicably abandoned by their crews. What drove them to it, nobody knows.

* * *

Ship's name: Hermania
Location: Cornish coast, south-west England
Date: 1849
Notes: Dutch ship. Evidence of gale damage (broken mast). Lifeboat still in place. Crew's belongings still in place. But no sign of crew.

* * *

Ship: Zebrina
Location: English Channel
Date: 1917
Notes: Left England for the short voyage to France. Two days later, found drifting and deserted. No signs of struggle or disturbance on board. No sign of crew.

Ship: <u>Belle Isle</u>
Location: Gulf of Lyon
Date: 1941
Notes: French cutter. Sails set and intact. Ship undamaged. No sign of crew. No clues whatsoever.

* * *

Ship: <u>Joyita</u>
Location: South Pacific
Date: 1955
Notes: In October left Western Samoa heading north. In November, found floundering and deserted. Despite its poor condition, the ship was known to be unsinkable because of its cork lining. The captain and crew were well aware of this. So why did they abandon ship? On further inspection, signs were found that two men had stayed on board for a while at least but they were now nowhere to be found. They had left behind a tent-like awning but whether it had been used as a sunshade or for collecting rainwater for drinking wasn't clear.

The ship was towed back to port in Fiji where she was pumped out. It was soon clear that she had suffered severe mechanical problems – a pipe in the boiler room had burst and flooded the ship. The investigators also discovered some blood-stained bandages which suggested that someone, maybe the captain, had been badly injured. Had he then given orders for the crew to abandon ship?

As far as anyone could tell, the following seems to be the most likely account of what happened: far out to sea, the ship's engines had stopped. The pipe in the boiler room had burst, causing serious flooding. The captain had been injured and issued the command for the rest of the crew and passengers to abandon ship. They had set sail in the lifeboats but had perished at sea. The captain had stayed on board, hence the awning, with one companion.

Which was all very well. But it didn't answer the most important questions, namely, what happened to the two men who stayed behind? Even if the captain had died of his wound, surely his companion might have survived? One suggestion was that the Joyita had been overtaken and boarded by a passing pirate ship and the two men murdered. As evidence, people pointed to the fact that several cases of cargo were missing, presumably plundered by the pirates. But it's much more likely that these were thrown overboard when the ship flooded, to try to lighten the load and stop her sinking. No really plausible explanation has ever been put forward. The mystery of the Joyita seems set to stay.

The curse of the laughing man

As she walked past the junk shop, something in the window caught Marie Lambert's eye – a tiny statue of a plump, half-naked man sitting cross-legged on a cushion. She recognized it at once – it was Ho-tei, the laughing man, the Japanese god of good luck. "I'll just pop inside and see how much they're asking for it," she told her husband. "It'll probably be far too expensive!" The place was the city of Kobe in Japan; the year, 1928. The Lamberts were enjoying the holiday of a lifetime – a cruise around the world. Mrs Lambert came out of the shop smiling broadly. She had bought the statue and was delighted with her purchase. It had cost far less than she had expected, even though it was made of real ivory, creamy-white and delicately carved. The only slight blemish was a tiny hole beneath the base, which had been plugged with an ivory peg and barely showed. A bargain, by anyone's standards.

The Lamberts made their way back to their ship – their next port of call Manila in the Philippines. It was then that the problems began. First, Mrs Lambert got toothache. She went to the ship's doctor who prescribed her some painkillers but they seemed to have very little effect at all. The ache got worse and worse, until it was a raging pain which kept Mrs Lambert awake at night and in agony during the day. It was two weeks before the ship was due to reach Manila, the first chance Mrs Lambert would have to consult a dentist. For the Lamberts, they were to be two very long weeks indeed. Eventually, the ship arrived in Manila. But, even before Mrs Lambert could go ashore, she and her husband were struck down by a mysterious fever which made every joint in their bodies ache. Worse was to come. When she had recovered sufficiently to be able to walk, Mrs Lambert finally made it to the dentist. So far, so good. But, for the first time in his long and highly respected career, the dentist's drill slipped and hit a nerve. The pain of the toothache had been bad enough but this was sheer agony!

The next stage of the voyage took them to Australia. And this time is was Mr Lambert's turn for misfortune. (It has to be said that, somehow during the voyage, the statue of the laughing man had slipped from Mrs Lambert's suitcase, where she had stored it, into that of her husband.) The day after they left Manila, he woke up with a terrible toothache. When he struggled to the dentist in Cairns, he was told that there was absolutely nothing wrong with his teeth. Uncannily, the toothache had stopped while he was in sitting in the dentist's chair (strange how this happens, isn't it!), but as soon as he was back on board ship, it returned with a vengeance. The same thing happened when he visited another dentist, a couple of days later. By the time they reached Brisbane, Mr Lambert had reached his wits' end. He ordered the dentist to pull out his teeth, one by one, until the pain stoppped. Reluctantly the dentist agreed – the teeth looked fine and healthy to him. He began to pull . . . And, guess what? As soon as the first tooth came out, the pain went away. Mr Lambert was delighted – first time lucky, he thought. Now, at last, he could look forward to rest of the cruise, free of pain. Not for long. The minute he set foot on the ship again, the toothache returned.

And so it continued, off and on, until the ship reached the United States. Whenever their luggage (containing the statue) was in their cabin, the toothache returned. On the few occasions when the luggage was stored somewhere else, the pain went away. Mrs Lambert's mother lived in the United States and the couple had been looking forward to visiting her before they returned to Britain.

They showed her all the souvenirs they had bought on the trip – including the statue of the god, Ho-tei. Mrs Lambert's mother was so taken by the statue that they decided to give it to her as a gift. A few hours later, her teeth began to ache – a familiar story by now – despite the fact that she had had excellent teeth all her life. She handed the statue back. "I don't know about bringing good luck," she said. "More like bad luck, I'd have said." The Lamberts were dismayed but they still did not put two and two together. It never crossed their minds that their recent misfortunes had anything at all to do with the statue.

The suspicion that there might, just might, be a link came as they sailed across the Atlantic on their way to Britain. They lent the statue to a fellow passenger who was interested in Japanese ivory carvings and wanted to show the figure to her husband. It was too late to return the statue to the Lamberts so she kept it in her cabin overnight. The next morning, both she and her husband had raging toothache. This set the Lamberts thinking – their own bouts of toothache had always coincided with the statue being in their cabin. And whenever someone else had had the statue in their possession, they had suffered the same fate while the Lamberts had been toothache free. Was it just coincidence? Or could there really be a link?

Mrs Lambert wanted to throw the statue overboard. "I want to be rid of the wretched thing," she told her husband. "Once and for all." But her husband stopped her just in time. He was worried that the statue might take some form of revenge on them if they tried to destroy it. The toothache was bad enough. Any retaliation might be a hundred times worse. So they took the statue back home to London with them where they showed it to an expert in Japanese art. The expert immediately offered them a large sum of money for it but the Lamberts refused. "We can't take money for it," Mr Lambert said, describing the catalogue of troubles it had caused. The expert sent for an elderly Japanese man who examined the statue carefully. He told them that statues of gods such as Ho-tei were often given "souls", in the form of tiny medallions hidden inside them. This might explain the ivory plug in the base of the statue which the Lamberts thought was to hide a blemish. The old Japanese man placed the statue in a shrine in a corner of the gallery, lit joss sticks in front of it, bowed in deep reverence and left.

The Lamberts left the statue where it was. They never went back to the gallery again.

Their mysterious aches and pains disappeared, never to return. The jinx was gone. So, had their troubles been pure bad luck? It seems hard to believe. Or could they be put down to the Japanese god who took revenge on those who removed him from his rightful place and homeland?

The house that hummed

The Binkowski family of New York, USA, were perfectly normal, fit and healthy until the day their house began to hum. Then, all of a sudden, they began to suffer a series of mysterious illnesses such as toothaches, earaches, frequent headaches, stiffness in the joints. They traced the source of their troubles to a faint humming sound which could heard throughout the house. They reported the problem to the police but nothing untoward could be found.

News of the humming sound spread fast and soon the state electricity company became interested. They sent investigators to the Binkowski's house, equipped with the latest in sound technology, and conducted a series of tests. But, in the end, they had to admit defeat. In their report, they said that they could hear no unusual sounds whatsoever anywhere in the house.

Mr Binkowski had reached the end of his tether. In utter despair, he wrote a letter to the President. It obviously made an impression. Some days later, a group of experts from the Air Force turned up, with even more sophisticated equipment at their disposal. Even they could not find the hum, though they did come to the conclusion that the whole Binkowski family had unusually sharp hearing. Yet many of the scores of visitors who descended on the Binkowski's home also reported hearing the hum. Eventually, the Binkowskis had had enough. They'd put up with the hum and its unpleasant side-effects for months on end. They finally decided to move out of the house and into a garage to escape from it once and for all.

Cursed cars

There are many reports of cars bringing disaster on whoever owned them. Was this coincidence? Or were they cursed? You'll have to make your own mind up!

A famous example of a cursed car is the one in which Archduke Francis Ferdinand of

Austria and Hungary and his wife were assassinated in 1914 – the event which led to the outbreak of the First World War. The car then came into the possession of an Austrian officer, General Potiorek. The car's bad luck continued. A few weeks later, General Potiorek's troops suffered a terrible defeat, for which the General was held directly responsible. He was sent back to Vienna, where, unable to bear the disgrace, he went mad and died.

The car's next owner was an Austrian captain who had served under General Potiorek's command. Less than a fortnight later, the captain was driving the car when he hit and killed two people, then swerved off the road and smashed into a tree. He died instantly of a broken neck.

The car, miraculously, survived the crash almost intact and, when the war ended, it was sold to the Governor of Yugoslavia. The catalogue of misfortune grew. The Governor, usually an extremely safe driver, had four accidents in as many months. In the worst of these, he lost an arm.

The car's next owners, and their fates, were as follows:

• A doctor – drove it into a ditch and was found crushed to death inside it.

• A jeweller – committed suicide shortly

afterwards.

- A racing driver – killed in a race in the Alps (while driving the jinxed car).
- A farmer – smashed the car into a horse and cart and turned it upside down.
- A garage owner – killed himself and four passengers while trying to overtake another car at high speed.
- A museum in Vienna – where it has been ever since!

The unluckiest ship in the world

Alongside cars, there are several contenders for the title of "Unluckiest Ship in the World". Among the favourites is the *Great Eastern*, a massive steamship built by the famous British engineer, Isambard Kingdom Brunel, and launched in 1858. Brunel's ambition was to build a ship so huge that it could travel around the world without having to stop to refuel. The *Great Eastern* lived up to its billing. It was enormous – almost 19,000 tonnes in weight and over 300 metres long, with room for 12,000 tonnes of coal (used as fuel) and living accommodation for four thousand passengers. At the time, she was the largest ship in the world.

She also proved to be the unluckiest. Misfortune dogged her building and launch. During the construction of the ship, a riveter and his young apprentice vanished without trace. The ship was so heavy that all the usual attempts to launch her failed, miserably. It eventually took three months and an army of hydraulic jacks to shift her from her berth. Worse was to follow. On her maiden voyage, Brunel himself collapsed on deck of a heart attack, and died. An valve through which steam escaped was accidentally left closed, causing a terrible explosion in which five men were burned to death. A whole host of accidents at sea, collisions and close-shaves were to follow the *Great Eastern* wherever she sailed.

Finally, only fifteen years after her trouble-laden launch, Brunel's gigantic dreamship was brought back to Britain where she languished and rusted and blocked up the shipping lanes. No one knew quite what to do with her. Eventually, in 1889, it was decided to break the *Great Eastern* up for scrap. Needless to say, this proved far, far easier said than done. A brand-new device, called the wrecker's ball (a huge iron ball hung on a gigantic chain) had to be invented – no other, existing piece of equipment was strong enough to do the job.

But what had caused all her misfortunes? Was it, once again, a case of coincidence, or was it something more mysterious than than? As the ship's double-thick hull was being demolished, some people thought the answer had been found. For here the demolition team discovered the skeletons of the riveter and his apprentice, who had disappeared fifteen years before. This, it was claimed, was the source of the ship's disastrous luck – a curse put upon by it by the souls of its very first casualties.

It's a miracle – or is it?

Great things are expected of two bottles of blood kept in Naples Cathedral, Italy. The blood they contain is thought to be that of St Januarius who was martyred for his Christian beliefs in AD 305. Three times a year, devotees claim, the dried black blood changes colour and becomes normal, red, liquid blood. This has happened thousands of times but always on three special feast days in May, September and December. From other churches come many reports of statues of the Virgin Mary (Christ's mother) which weep tears of blood. No evidence of trickery, however clever, has ever been found despite numerous tests and investigations. So is it a miracle?

· The doll with the human hair

A pottery doll growing real human hair? Surely not? But stranger things have happened . . .

In 1938, a man called Eikichi Suzuki took a pottery doll to a temple in the village of Monji-Saiwai Cho in northern Japan. He wanted to place the doll in the temple for safe-keeping. It had been the most precious possession of his sister, Kiku, who had died years before at three years of age. Since her death, he had looked after the doll and kept it in a box with his dead sister's ashes. But the Second World War was not far off and Eikichi knew he would be called up to fight. The temple was the safest place to leave the doll that he could think of.

Eikichi was not able to return to the temple until nine years later. The doll had indeed been kept safe and sound, and the priest now handed the box back to its owner. With the priest standing close by, Eikichi opened the box . . . He could not believe his eyes! In his absence, the doll's hair had grown, right down to her shoulders. More astonishing still, it was human hair!

The priest placed the doll back in the shrine, where its incredible hair continued to grow. How or why, nobody knows but it still keeps on growing. Pilgrims flock from far and wide to witness this miracle, believing the doll to be a link with the Buddha himself. According to the priest, the growing hair is a sign that Kiku's soul somehow lives on through her treasured doll.

· Miracle worker or magician?

But miracles are not confined to bottles of blood or dolls with human hair. There are many human examples of miracle-workers — people able to cure the sick or raise the dead with a touch, a word or by their mere presence. The following extraordinary chain of events occurred in Paris, France, in May 1727. The occasion was the funeral of a young deacon, Francois de Paris.

Francois de Paris belonged to a religious order called the Jansenists. They denied the existence of human free will. Only God's divine grace could save sinners from sin. In his relatively short life, Francois de Paris had made quite a name for himself. He was well known (and respected) for his spartan lifestyle and for his charitable work with the poor. It all proved too much for him and he died from a combination of exhaustion and near starvation. Hundreds of mourners attended his funeral and filed past his coffin which was placed behind the altar in St Medard's church.

The procession of mourners began quietly and calmly enough. Then some very strange things began to happen. A small boy with a twisted leg, limped past with his father. He could only walk with the greatest difficulty but he had pleaded not to be left at home. In his hand he clutched a bunch of flowers. As he stopped to place the flowers on the coffin, he suddenly fell to the ground, rolling and writhing on the floor as if he were having some sort of fit. A few moments later, the boy sat up, looked around and asked his father to help him up. The fit had passed. But as he got to his feet, he began to laugh and shout for joy. "My leg! My leg!" he cried. "It's better! Oh, look!" And sure enough, the crippled leg was as good as new, and the boy could walk quite normally, for the first time in his life. "It's a miracle!" his father exclaimed. And so it seemed to be.

Other people wanted a miracle too. They surged forward to touch the coffin, convinced it would cure them of their ills. A woman with a paralysed arm was cured; a blind person was able to see once again. When the coffin was finally moved from the church and buried in the nearby graveyard, the miracles continued. One woman with cancer was completely cured – her doctors confessed they could now find nothing wrong with her at all, despite the fact that days before she had been at death's door.

But it was another, even stranger, series of events which began to worry the authorities. Dozens of people who visited the tomb experience extraordinary convulsions. During these fits they seemed to feel no pain, and even begged people to beat them with sticks or hammers. Some could stick their hands into fire and pull them out unburnt. One man could leap high into the air, even though he was tied with heavy iron chains. Another could spin very fast on one leg, while reading the Bible. It was all very odd.

Eventually, the authorities clamped down – events at the tomb were becoming an embarrassment and awkward questions were being asked. Five years after the deacon's death, they closed down the graveyard and the miracles stopped. No explanation of what happened was ever found. Of course there were doubters. But there were others who, convinced that the whole thing was a fraud, changed their minds once they saw what went on.

The girl with green skin

Farmers working in the field near the small Spanish village of Banjos one fine August day in 1887 could not believe their eyes. Out of a nearby cave walked two children – a boy and a girl, with skin as green as the farmers' crops.

The children could not speak any Spanish and none of the villagers could understand their language. Apart from green skin, they had almond-shaped eyes and were wearing clothes made from a material which had never been seen in Spain before. The farmers took them back to the village and gave them some food. But the children would not eat it. For almost a week, the villagers tried to tempt them to eat but to no avail. Finally, they began to eat some beans. But the boy was so weakened by lack of food, he very soon died. The girl survived but the bright green colour of her skin gradually faded away.

The girl was quick to learn and soon could speak enough Spanish to tell the villagers some of her story. But it was almost too strange to believe. She told them that the country she came from had no sunshine, though the land across the river was very warm and sunny. She had lived there very happily until, one day, a very strong wind had lifted her and her brother into the air and carried them into the cave.

Five years later the girl died. And the mystery of who she was, where she came from and of her green skin went with her.

Not so sweet dreams

One April night in 1865, the president of the USA, Abraham Lincoln had a very disturbing dream. In the dream, he was lying asleep in his bedroom in the White House (as he indeed was). He woke up suddenly, roused from his sleep by the sound of people weeping loudly. Lincoln got up and followed the sound into the East Room. There he saw a procession of people filing past a coffin. They were paying their last respects and were, quite clearly, deeply distressed. But whose death was being mourned? Lincoln could not see the corpse's face so he asked one of the guards who was dead. The answer horrified him.

"It's the President," the soldier said. "He's been assassinated."

At this terrifying point, Lincoln woke up. He told his wife and several friends about the dream, relieved that it was nothing more. He was wrong. Later that month, Lincoln went to

the theatre for a rare night out. As he settled down to enjoy the evening, an assassin pulled out his gun and shot him. . .

Out of body experience

In his book, *The Romeo Error*, biologist Lyall Watson tells the astonishing tale of his own "out of body" experience. It occurred in the early 1970s when he was on safari, driving through the Kenyan bush. Suddenly the minibus he was travelling in skidded and turned upside down. It then rolled several times before coming to rest at the edge of a gully.

A couple of minutes passed. The next thing that Lyall Watson knew was that he was standing outside the minibus, looking towards it. The strange thing was that, inside the minibus, he could clearly see his own body sprawled across the front seat, knocked unconscious by the crash. Then a more pressing problem caught his attention. When the minibus had finally come to a stop, a young boy had been pushed up through the bus' canvas roof. His head and shoulders were now sticking out. The minibus was balanced precariously on the very edge of the gully. If it toppled over, the boy would be crushed underneath it as it fell.

Almost at the same moment as this thought crossed his mind, Watson's real body began to regain consciousness. From where he lay, he could not actually see the boy but his memory of the scene he had witnessed was vivid. At once, he climbed through the window of the minibus and pulled the boy free. Just in time. Barely minutes later, the minibus crashed over the edge.

Watson was in no doubt that somehow his

body and mind had become detached from each other. But he was at a loss to explain how this had happened.

Revenge of the spirits

Despite a 24-hour police guard no reason could be found for a series of attacks on a block of flats in Hamilton, New Zealand. During the attacks, some of which lasted for four hours, glass bottles and jars were hurled at the flats until the area was thick with broken glass. It was up to a group of Maori elders to explain the mystery. They said that the flats had been built on a piece of sacred land – the spirits were simply taking their revenge.

Mind over matter

Wolf Messing was no stranger to danger. A Jew, he had fled for his life from Poland during the Second World War and made his way to Russia. He had another good reason for seeking sanctuary – Adolf Hitler had put a price on his head. For Messing was a mind reader by profession and had dared to predict Hitler's downfall and death.

Now he faced another challenge – Stalin heard about his claims and set him a test. Messing was to gain entry into Stalin's country house – one of the most closely guarded buildings in Europe – without a pass. Stalin, it has to be said, was confident that Messing would fail.

Imagine then his surprise when, one fine day, he was sitting at his desk in his country house and a man strolled nonchalantly across the garden, into the house and straight into Stalin's office where he calmly sat down in a chair. It was none other than Messing! Stalin was amazed – how on earth had he got past the guards? Indeed, why had the guards and servants stood back so respectfully as he had passed?

Messing explained. He had made the guards think that he was a man called Lavrenti Beria, the much-feared chief of the secret police. No wonder he wasn't stopped! Messing looked nothing like Beria but so great were his powers of persuasion, nobody questioned him.

The missing link?

Franek Klusky was a Polish medium, made famous by a series of seances he held in 1920.

Also present were several researchers from the International Metaphysical Institute, who kept a close eye on Klusky throughout to check on any trickery.

The group of people gathered for the seance sat in a circle and linked hands. Klusky concentrated harder and harder. Suddenly, the large, looming shape of a mysterious creature appeared among the sitters. It was about as tall as a man but hairy like an ape, with ape-like features and long, swinging arms. It had a smell of damp dog about it. One sitter put out a hand towards it, which it licked with its large tongue!

The sitters, including the researchers, were utterly convinced by what they had seen. They had complete faith in Klusky's psychic powers. Other people weren't so sure . . .

Do vampires exist?

The vampires of stories and legends are supernatural beings, the living dead, who sleep by day and only venture abroad at night. Then they change from human form to that of a bat. They convert other people, their innocent victims, into vampires by sucking the blood from their necks.

The most famous vampire is, of course, Count Dracula, created by the novelist Bram Stoker in 1897. But was Count Dracula purely a work of fiction? Or did he actually exist? Stoker seems to have based his character on a real-life Rumanian prince, Vlad IV, also known as Vlad the Impaler who lived in the fifteenth century. He was a great, and greatly feared, military leader but his claim to fame, and his name, came from the gruesome way he dealt with prisoners of war. The unfortunate victims were impaled on sharp poles and Vlad was said to get great pleasure from watching them writhing in agony. But whether he was in fact a vampire, or a ruthless psychopath, no one knows.

Whether fact or fiction, the fear of vampires still exists. In 1973, a Polish man was found dead in his flat in central England. He had choked to death on a clove of garlic which he'd put into his mouth last thing at night. Salt was sprinkled over his bed and a bowl of urine mixed with garlic stood on the bedroom windowsill. All classic remedies for warding off vampires . . .

ALSO FROM ROBINSON CHILDREN'S BOOKS

True Horror Stories   Terrance Dicks   **£4.99** { }
Fact is stranger than fiction and often more chilling. The spine-tingling stories
in this book are true, but some will be the most frightening you have ever
encountered!

Space Stories   Ed. Mike Ashley   **£4.99** { }
Over 30 exciting and intriguing space adventures – some take place on a
future Earth, some in our solar system, and some on worlds far away.

Fantasy Stories   Ed. Mike Ashley   **£4.99** { }
Brings together some of the most imaginative fantasy stories this century,
some written especially for this book, others already classics.

Horse Stories   Ed. Felicity Trotman   **£4.99** { }
Wonderful new stories by Monica Edwards, Andrew Lang, and Geraldine
McCaughrean, as well as modern classics by such popular writers as James
Herriot.

Dance Stories   Ed. Felicity Trotman   **£6.99** { }
Exciting, glamorous and romantic stories about the world of dance, from over
thirty top authors.

Robinson Publishing Ltd, PO Box 11, Falmouth, Cornwall TR10 9EN
Tel:+44(0)1326317200 Fax: +44(0)1326317444
Email:books@Barni.avel.co.uk

UK/BFPO customers please allow £1.00 for p&p for the first book, plus 50p
for the second, plus 30p for each additional book up to a maximum charge of
£3.00. Overseas customers (inc Ireland) please allow £2.00 for the first book,
plus £1.00 for the second, plus 50p for each additional book.

Please send me the titles ticked above.

NAME (Block letters) _____

ADDRESS _____

_____

_____ POSTCODE_____

I enclose a cheque/PO (payable to Robinson Publishing Ltd) for_____

I wish to pay by Switch/Credit card _____

_____ Card Expiry Date _____